Prince Charles & Princess Diana

Prince Charles &
Princess Diana

Portrait of a Family

Prince Charles & Princess Diana

Portrait of a Family

Michèle Brown

METHUEN

Contents

The Royal Descent of The Princess of Wales

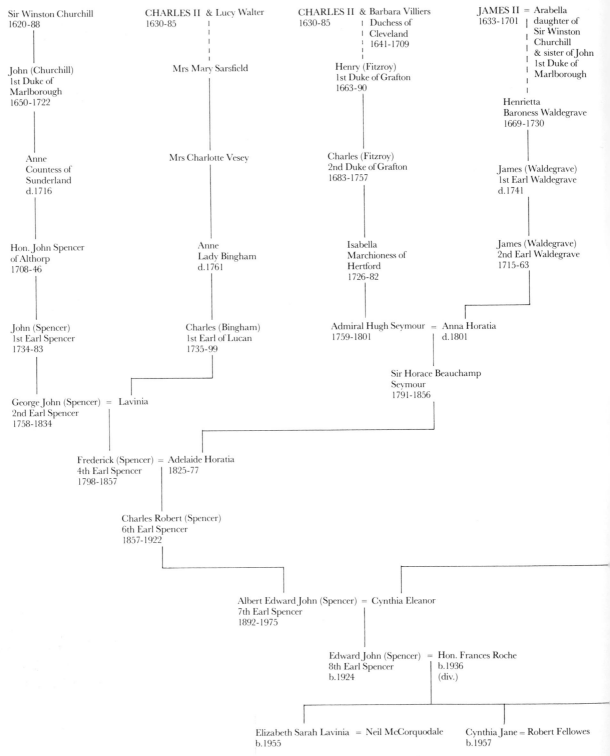

Sir Winston Churchill
1620-88

John (Churchill)
1st Duke of
Marlborough
1650-1722

Anne
Countess of
Sunderland
d.1716

Hon. John Spencer
of Althorp
1708-46

John (Spencer)
1st Earl Spencer
1734-83

CHARLES II & Lucy Walter
1630-85

Mrs Mary Sarsfield

Mrs Charlotte Vesey

Anne
Lady Bingham
d.1761

Charles (Bingham)
1st Earl of Lucan
1735-99

CHARLES II & Barbara Villiers
1630-85   Duchess of
              Cleveland
              1641-1709

Henry (Fitzroy)
1st Duke of Grafton
1663-90

Charles (Fitzroy)
2nd Duke of Grafton
1683-1757

Isabella
Marchioness of
Hertford
1726-82

Admiral Hugh Seymour = Anna Horatia
1759-1801   d.1801

JAMES II = Arabella
1633-1701   daughter of
            Sir Winston
            Churchill
            & sister of John
            1st Duke of
            Marlborough

Henrietta
Baroness Waldegrave
1669-1730

James (Waldegrave)
1st Earl Waldegrave
d.1741

James (Waldegrave)
2nd Earl Waldegrave
1715-63

Sir Horace Beauchamp
Seymour
1791-1856

George John (Spencer) = Lavinia
2nd Earl Spencer
1758-1834

Frederick (Spencer) = Adelaide Horatia
4th Earl Spencer   1825-77
1798-1857

Charles Robert (Spencer)
6th Earl Spencer
1857-1922

Albert Edward John (Spencer) = Cynthia Eleanor
7th Earl Spencer
1892-1975

Edward John (Spencer) = Hon. Frances Roche
8th Earl Spencer   b.1936
b.1924   (div.)

Elizabeth Sarah Lavinia = Neil McCorquodale
b.1955

Cynthia Jane = Robert Fellowes
b.1957

4

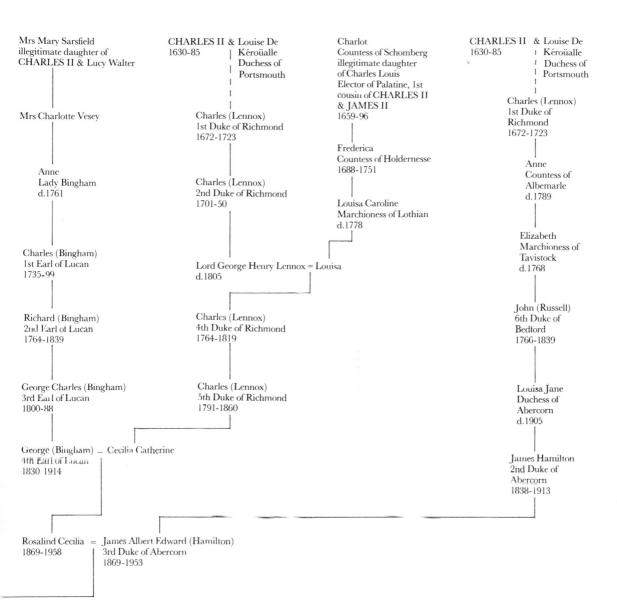

Mrs Mary Sarsfield
illegitimate daughter of
CHARLES II & Lucy Walter
|
Mrs Charlotte Vesey
|
Anne
Lady Bingham
d.1761
|
Charles (Bingham)
1st Earl of Lucan
1735-99
|
Richard (Bingham)
2nd Earl of Lucan
1764-1839
|
George Charles (Bingham)
3rd Earl of Lucan
1800-88
|
George (Bingham) — Cecilia Catherine
4th Earl of Lucan
1830-1914
|
Rosalind Cecilia = James Albert Edward (Hamilton)
1869-1958   3rd Duke of Abercorn
                   1869-1953

CHARLES II & Louise De
1630-85   Kéroüalle
                 Duchess of
                 Portsmouth
|
Charles (Lennox)
1st Duke of Richmond
1672-1723
|
Charles (Lennox)
2nd Duke of Richmond
1701-50
|
Lord George Henry Lennox = Louisa
d.1805
|
Charles (Lennox)
4th Duke of Richmond
1764-1819
|
Charles (Lennox)
5th Duke of Richmond
1791-1860

Charlot
Countess of Schomberg
illegitimate daughter
of Charles Louis
Elector of Palatine, 1st
cousin of CHARLES II
& JAMES II
1659-96
|
Frederica
Countess of Holdernesse
1688-1751
|
Louisa Caroline
Marchioness of Lothian
d.1778

CHARLES II & Louise De
1630-85   Kéroüalle
                 Duchess of
                 Portsmouth
|
Charles (Lennox)
1st Duke of
Richmond
1672-1723
|
Anne
Countess of
Albemarle
d.1789
|
Elizabeth
Marchioness of
Tavistock
d.1768
|
John (Russell)
6th Duke of
Bedford
1766-1839
|
Louisa Jane
Duchess of
Abercorn
d.1905
|
James Hamilton
2nd Duke of
Abercorn
1838-1913

Diana Frances
b. 1961

Charles Edward Maurice
Viscount Althorp
b.1964

5

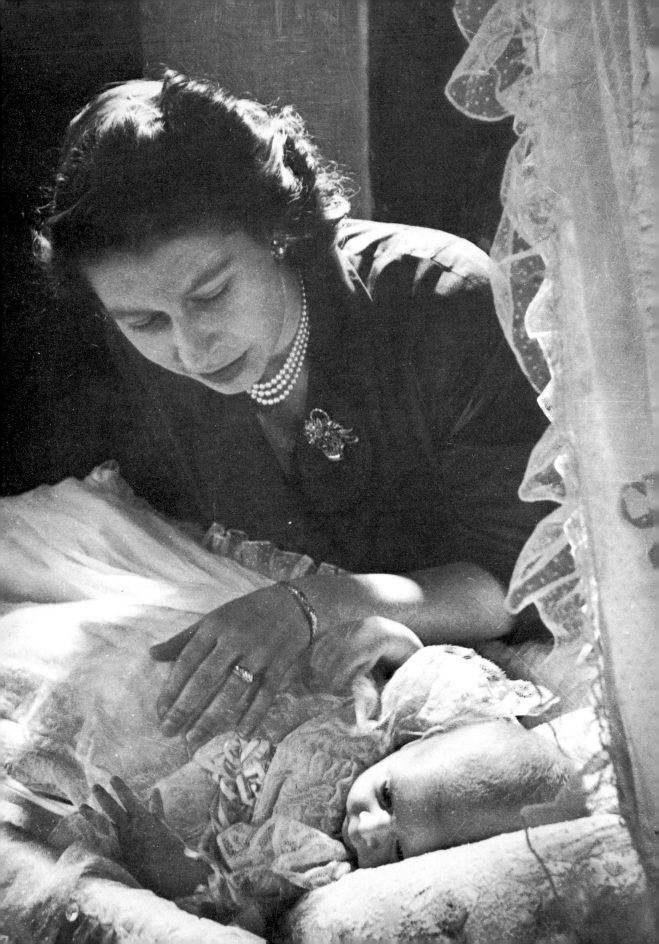

1

The First Three Years

Sunday, 14 November 1948 dawned cold and wet. Over the City of London the dank, winter morning hung like a shroud enveloping the bomb-sites and partially demolished buildings, visible scars of the war that had ended three years before.

However, neither the weather nor the drab austerity of post-war life could diminish the sense of excited expectation that gripped the crowd of Londoners clustered outside the railings of Buckingham Palace.

Since the summer the nation and the Commonwealth had been eagerly expecting a royal birth. A brief official statement that Princess Elizabeth, the Duchess of Edinburgh, would cease public engagements from the beginning of July had set the rumours flying. Now, in the middle of November, six days before her first wedding anniversary, the waiting was almost over.

During the previous weeks discreet preparations had been taking place inside Buckingham Palace. The Buhl Room, on the first floor overlooking the Mall, had been converted into a surgical theatre. Another room had been transformed into a nursery, and the royal midwife, Miss Helen Rowe, was now in residence. But it was the news that a leading gynaecologist, Sir William Gilliat, had spent the previous night in the Palace that heralded the long-awaited event and drew the crowds to the Palace gates early on that bitter Sunday morning.

By late afternoon a throng of several thousand was waiting outside the Palace. At teatime their hopes were raised by the sudden arrival of a fleet of cars carrying the King's physician and two other specialists to assist Sir William. This, the crowds knew, could mean only one thing.

The expectant father, the Duke of Edinburgh, naturally felt the mounting tension more keenly than anyone else. To work off his nervous energy he went to play squash in the Palace courts with Michael Parker, his friend from the Royal Navy and now his private secretary.

They were still exhausting themselves at 9.15 when Sir Alan Lascelles, the King's private secretary, rushed down with the news that a Prince had been born. Dashing upstairs, Philip found Elizabeth still sleeping under the anaesthetic she had been

OPPOSITE *The newly born Prince photographed by Cecil Beaton at Buckingham Palace a few weeks after the birth. Beaton noted afterwards that Prince Charles looked very like his grandmother, Queen Mary.*

The official bulletin announcing Prince Charles's safe arrival contrasts noticeably with the uninhibited tone of the newspaper headlines and the photograph of the enthusiastic crowd outside Buckingham Palace.

given for a forceps delivery, and in the nursery he took his first glimpse of his newly born son and heir.

When the Princess awoke, she was met by the sight of her husband smiling down at her and holding a bouquet of roses and carnations in his hand. Later he poured champagne for members of the household staff and the medical team in the adjoining room.

Meanwhile the Palace post office was already busy sending off hundreds of pre-prepared telegrams to British ambassadors and foreign heads of state around the globe. By ancient custom, the first of these was carried a somewhat shorter distance to be delivered by courier to the Lord Mayor of London.

In all the family's excitement and celebration, however, the faithful crowds packing the approaches to the Palace were not overlooked. An outside door was seen to open on the ground floor. The silhouetted figure of a man walked across the courtyard to the railings. Those pressed to the front saw him whispering to a policeman who had been trying to keep the crowds back from the gates. The officer turned to face the crowd, cupped his hands around his mouth and bellowed above their heads: 'It's a boy!'

Immediately the news was taken up around the Palace in a deafening roar that lasted for several hours, interrupted only by choruses of 'For he's a jolly good fellow' and 'We Want Philip'. Throughout the capital and the nation the news spread like wildfire. The fountains in Trafalgar Square were turned blue (for a boy) and continued so for a week. Across the country numerous bonfires flickered into life, guns were fired in salute, and in pubs throughout the land toasts were offered to the newborn Prince.

The news of his birth was conveyed formally to the crowds outside the Palace by an official bulletin written by Richard Colville, the King's press secretary. It read: 'Her Royal Highness the Princess Elizabeth was safely delivered of a Prince at 9.14 o'clock this evening. Her Royal Highness and the infant Prince are both doing well.' Typed notices, bearing the same message and signed by the Home Secretary, James Chuter Ede, were pinned to the doors of the Home Office in Whitehall and those of the Mansion House in the City.

An hour and a quarter after his birth, the infant Prince was visited by his great-grandmother, Queen Mary. Though still recovering from a recent attack of influenza, the elderly Queen was so heartened by her grand-daughter's news that she immediately summoned her car and drove up to Buckingham Palace from her home in Marlborough House.

In spite of her recent illness and the late hour, Queen Mary stayed with her son's family until well after midnight, by which time the happy but exhausted young mother was in need of rest. At her request two Palace officials went out to speak to the crowds whose well-meaning choruses and cheering were keeping her awake. However, their efforts failed to produce any notable reduction in the volume of their well-wishing, and eventually a police car was brought in to nose its way gently through the crowd repeating time and again through its loud-speaker: 'Ladies and gentlemen, it is requested from the Palace that we have a little quietness, if you please.' This message, the cold night air and the gradual extinguishing of lights inside the Palace, finally persuaded the crowds that the time had come to return home to their beds and allow the Royal Family to retire to theirs.

The morning after the birth of the Prince, messages of congratulation began to pour into the Palace from around the globe. The British fleet was dressed overall. Forty-one gun salutes boomed out in the former dominions of the Empire, members of the then recently constituted British Commonwealth. Flags and bunting festooned public and private buildings alike, while in London the bells of St Paul's Cathedral and Westminster Abbey led those of churches the length and breadth of the land in pealing their welcome to the baby, who was destined to become the Supreme Head of the Church in England.

Buckingham Palace was showered with letters and presents from around the world, and a dozen temporary typists had to be employed to answer the volume of correspondence. The BBC commissioned a suite entitled *Music for a Prince* from three of the foremost contemporary British composers, and the Poet Laureate, John Masefield, captured the general feeling of optimism that surrounded the infant Prince in his four lines of official verse, 'A Hope for the Newly-Born':

> May destiny, allotting what befalls,
>   Grant to the newly-born this saving grace,
> A guard more sure than ships and fortress-walls,
>   The loyal love and service of a race.

When the baby was a week old, the household staff were permitted a glimpse of the new arrival in the family, and this privilege was later accorded to certain Privy Councillors. But apart from these no other visitors were allowed to intrude on the privacy of the young royal couple and their first baby.

The Princess breast-fed her son for several weeks, during which time he slept in her dressing-room in a wicker basket that had once been used by Queen Victoria's children. By the time she left her bed, ten days after the delivery, her baby had already ventured out of doors to be pushed around the gardens of Buckingham Palace in a pram that had formerly conveyed his mother and aunt Margaret when they were his age.

Outside the Palace walls, however, the world at large was still agog for information about the royal baby. No photograph of him had yet been issued, and there was still no hint of the name by which he would become so well known. Those snippets of information that were released were instantly seized upon by the media. The Queen's sister, Countess Granville, speaking to a gathering of Girl Guides in Northern Ireland, divulged that the baby 'could not be more angelic looking. He is golden-haired and has the most beautiful complexion, as well as amazingly delicate features for so young a baby.' But apart from this and a few casual remarks made by

15 December 1948. Sister Helen Rowe takes the sleeping Prince from the arms of his grandmother to return him to the nursery after his christening.

other members of the immediate family to their close friends, very little was known about the baby until his christening on 15 December, a month after his birth.

Although at the time some voices of criticism were raised at this uncustomary delay, it can now be appreciated that this was the first of many measures taken by the Princess and her husband to protect their offspring from the glare of publicity that would inevitably surround their lives. In fact even before his birth their first son had been the cause of the ending of one archaic royal tradition. George VI had decided that the time had come to abolish the three-hundred-year-old custom that required a Minister of the Crown to attend and verify each royal birth. The king rightly felt that the centuries-old custom had little relevance to the royal House of

Windsor in the middle of the twentieth century. Princess Elizabeth thus became the first royal mother in nearly three hundred years not to have the embarrassing presence of a comparative stranger at her confinement, and James Chuter Ede became the first Home Secretary to be relieved of the uncomfortable duty of having to wait uneasily at one end of the room, while the royal birth took place at the other. He, like his successors, merely waited at the end of a telephone line for news of the birth, before signing the official bulletins.

There was considerable surprise, however, when it was revealed that another custom had been abandoned. The infant Prince was to be christened Charles Philip Arthur George. 'Charles' had, of course, been the name of two of the Stuart kings as well as of the Young Pretender who had led the Scottish rebellion against the Prince's ancestors in the middle of the eighteenth century. But 'Albert', the name of Queen Victoria's consort, had been omitted, although Queen Victoria had expressly desired that all her male descendants should bear his name. Princess Margaret, on hearing the eventual choice of name, remarked with her usual wry sense of humour that she would probably be known thereafter as 'Charlie's Aunt'. It was quite clear though that the Duke and Duchess of Edinburgh had chosen the names which they liked best, and these were registered by the Duke with the senior registrar of Caxton Hall in the City of Westminster, on the morning of the baby's christening.

The christening, like the registration, took place at Buckingham Palace. Since the Palace chapel had still not been repaired after being destroyed by wartime bombing, the service was held in the White Drawing-room, overlooking the wintry Palace

Windlesham Moor, Surrey, the house used by Princess Elizabeth and the Duke of Edinburgh before they established themselves at Clarence House.

gardens. Although Queen Victoria's wish regarding the Prince's name had been set aside, her presence was still evident at the service. The baby was dressed in the robe of Honiton lace and white silk which had been worn by all Queen Victoria's children and later by the future George VI, the baby's mother and his aunt. In addition he was baptized in the Lily Font which had been made for the christening of the first of Queen Victoria's children. This had been brought to London from Windsor, where royal christenings usually took place, and had been filled with water from the River Jordan, in accordance with a royal custom that dates back to the Crusades.

Displaying his now familiar ceremonial dignity, even at the tender age of one month, Prince Charles entered the Church of England without a whimper as the Archbishop of Canterbury baptized him. During the half-hour-long service the baby was held by his youngest godparent, Princess Margaret.

In spite of the celebrations and the customary congratulations, the ceremony was overhung by an atmosphere of worry and apprehension. Only two days after the Prince's birth it had been announced that the King had been forced to cancel a scheduled tour of the Commonwealth as a result of his ailing health. Although it was hoped that he would respond to treatment in due course, his doctors advised him against travelling even as far as Windsor for the traditional family Christmas. So for the first time in many years the Royal Family spent the festive season at Buckingham Palace.

The responsibility of looking after the young Prince passed from Sister Helen Rowe to two Scottish-born nurses, Helen Lightbody and Mabel Anderson. Miss Lightbody, who was always given the courtesy title of 'Mrs' as the senior of the two, was already known to the Princess. She had previously been engaged in bringing up the sons of the Duke of Gloucester. Miss Anderson, who was still in her early twenties, had placed an advertisement in the 'Situations Wanted' column of a nurses' magazine. To her amazement she found herself not only invited to the Palace for an interview but subsequently offered the job by the Princess. This proved to be a highly successful appointment, since Miss Anderson went on to take charge of all Her Majesty's children and later became nanny to her first grandchild, Peter Phillips. So, with the nannies appointed, the young household was complete, for the time being. All they needed was a home of their own.

Before their son's birth, the Duke and Duchess of Edinburgh had lived in a rented house at Windlesham, but as the lease on that home had almost expired, the King had decided to set them up in Clarence House. However, with skilled builders at a premium because of the extensive wartime destruction, the restoration work and conversions that were needed took much longer than expected. In fact it was not until the beginning of July 1949 that the young couple were able to move from the six-hundred-room Palace to their own elegant town-house.

Originally a large rambling royal residence, Clarence House had been coverted into the offices of the British Red Cross Society during the war. Now renovated as a

Prince Charles being taken on his customary morning walk around St James's Park by Nanny Lightbody on his second birthday. Later, the attentions of the public caused these outings to be made to more remote London parks.

modern family home, much of its daily activity was centred around the pale blue, chintz-curtained nursery that overlooked the secluded square garden and St James's Park beyond.

Every day one of the two nurses would take Prince Charles for a walk. Frequently they would venture beyond the walled garden to enjoy the wider spaces of one of the London parks. Wearing ordinary nursing uniforms and pushing a seemingly anonymous baby, they ran little risk of being identified and attracting undue public attention, though a detective was always at hand a few paces behind just to be on the safe side.

From time to time the young Prince would be taken to visit his great-grandmother in nearby Marlborough House. The sight of the baby playing at her feet must have brought great happiness to Queen Mary's declining years. She had survived the death of her husband and two of her sons. She had seen another son abdicate the throne and go into exile, and she now knew that a third son had only a short time to live. Perhaps it was the future hopes that she rested in the infant Charles that prompted her to let him play with the valuable jade and crystal objects in her priceless collection. Certainly she had never been so relaxed with her own children, and Charles's mother and Princess Margaret had never been allowed to touch any of the precious ornaments when they were his age. For the Prince's own part, one of his earliest memories is of 'Gan-Gan', as he called Queen Mary, as a large person sitting

Clarence House, where Princess Elizabeth and the Duke of Edinburgh lived until they moved into Buckingham Palace, a few months after the Princess's accession to the throne.

bolt upright with her feet resting on a foot-stool surrounded by display-cabinets full of glittering objects.

By the time Charles was one year old, his parents had resumed their normal working routine. Prince Philip had returned to the Royal Navy and was serving in the Mediterranean, while Princess Elizabeth was increasingly called upon to attend official functions in place of her ailing father.

The Prince's supremacy as his parents' only child lasted a mere twenty-one months, coming to an end with the birth of his sister, Princess Anne, on 15 August 1950. The day was doubly important for the Duke of Edinburgh, since he was gazetted a lieutenant-commander on the same date and subsequently received his first command, the frigate HMS *Magpie*, which was on service in the Mediterranean.

At Christmas Princess Elizabeth flew to join her husband in Malta while the two children stayed with their grandparents and spent their first Christmas at Sandringham. The King, whose health had apparently improved, was evidently delighted with his grandchildren, and his grandson in particular, who had just started to walk. Writing to his daughter he said: 'Charles is too sweet, stumping around the room. We shall love having him at Sandringham. He is the fifth generation to live there, and I hope he will get to like the place.'

Re-united with their mother once more, the children settled back into an orderly daily routine. In spite of her royal duties and their father's absence at sea, they probably saw as much of their parents as children in any other household employing nannies. Both parents were determined to spend as much time with them as they could. The Princess set aside certain periods of her day to spend exclusively with the children. So in spite of having two busy working parents, whose duties often took them away from home, Charles and Anne were brought up in the secure comfort of a well-regulated, loving household.

They were up sharp at seven every morning to be washed, dressed and given breakfast. After this they played in the nursery until it was time for the first visit to their mother at nine o'clock. Half an hour later they left her to her work and went for a morning walk that lasted until midday. Lunch was served at one o'clock – which, as far as Charles was concerned, was not a minute too soon. After a rest the two children spent the afternoon playing in the garden or visiting the Queen or their great-grandmother, Queen Mary. After tea they spent another period of the day with their mother (and their father too when he was at home), playing on the nursery floor and enjoying the fun and games of bath-time, before being tucked up after their bedtime story.

Although like any other little boy, Charles was happy in his own secure world of parental adoration, and free to enjoy nursery-rhymes like 'Pop Goes the Weasel' and favourite meals of boiled chicken and rice, the differences between his life and that of other children were apparent even at this early age.

The afternoon walks in the central London parks began to attract crocodiles of curious observers, so that the royal children were often taken further afield, to Richmond Park or Wimbledon Common, where they could enjoy greater freedom from public attention. In other, more unusual, respects their upbringing had to differ from that of other toddlers. Charles learned to bow whenever he went to see his great-grandmother; he was taught not to sit down in the presence of his grandfather until asked to do so, and both royal children were made to stand still for long periods as training for the many ceremonies and official functions they would attend in later life.

The King's deteriorating health, which had already been putting greater demands on his daughter's time, eventually forced Prince Philip reluctantly to relinquish his naval command in July 1951, so that he could assist his wife in carrying out her increased public duties. Three months later they delayed their departure for a tour of North America while the King underwent a major operation. Even though this surgery was successful, it had revealed a far greater cause for concern, and when the Princess and her husband finally left for Montreal, she carried with her an envelope containing the official papers that she would have to sign in the event of the King's dying while she was still abroad. The reason for this was the secret knowledge that she shared with her mother and the doctors that her father was dying of cancer.

OPPOSITE *A cover of* Illustrated Magazine *showing the young Royal Family with its latest addition, Princess Anne, who was born on 15 August 1950. Prince Philip was still a full-time Naval Officer, based in Malta.*

WEEK ENDING FEBRUARY 17 1951   EVERY WEDNESDAY THREEPENCE

ILLUSTRATED

The Young Royal Family

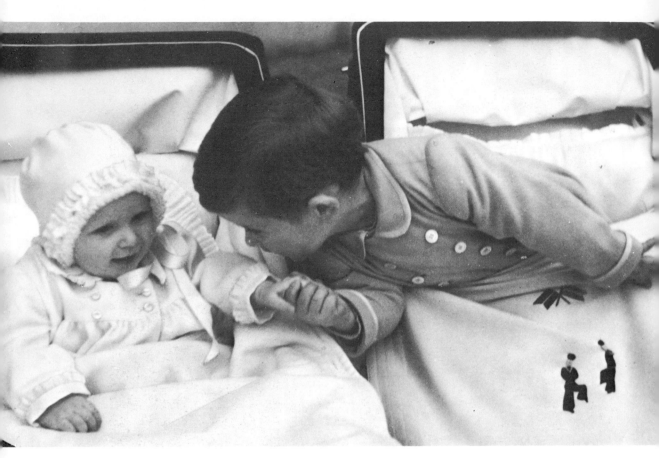

Prince Charles shows a little brotherly tenderness towards his sister as they are both wheeled out in their capacious prams.

With his parents away, Charles spent his third birthday with his grandparents, his sister and his aunt Margaret at Buckingham Palace. This was the occasion that is recorded in the now famous photograph taken of him with his grandfather. The Prince still has an impression of sitting beside someone much larger while another person swung something shiny in front of him. This was the press secretary, Richard Colville, who was trying to attract the little boy's attention long enough for the photograph to be taken. This picture has always held a special significance in Her Majesty's affections, linking as it does one of her last memories of her father with one of the first portraits of her eldest son.

When Charles's parents returned for Christmas, however, it was only to inform their disappointed children that they would have to be off again in the very near future. This time they were due to undertake the tour of the Commonwealth that had been postponed shortly after Charles's birth. The night before the Prince and Princess were due to leave, the King took them to see the musical *South Pacific* at Drury Lane: it was the first time he had been to the theatre for several months. The

As well as the immediate family this picture taken at Sandringham shows (back row) the Duke of Kent, Princess Alexandra, the Duchess of Kent, the Duke and Duchess of Gloucester and (front row) Prince Richard of Gloucester, Prince Michael of Kent and Prince William of Gloucester.

following morning he drove with them to London Airport to see them off on the first leg of their journey, a flight to Africa. As the plane taxied away, the Princess saw his frail, drawn figure standing on the windswept tarmac, bravely waving goodbye. She fastened her seat-belt and took off from English soil for the last time as a Princess.

King George VI bore himself with characteristic courage and steadfastness to the end. He spent 5 February 1952 in a successful day's shooting at Sandringham. After writing notes thanking those who had helped organize the day's sport, he enjoyed a relaxing meal with his wife and younger daughter, after which he spent an hour and a half reading papers at his desk before turning in. That night he died in his sleep.

The following morning Charles and Anne noticed that something was wrong as they had been made to stay in the nursery for longer than usual, instead of being taken to see Granny. Eventually Charles asked his nanny why so many of the servants seemed to be crying, only to be told by Miss Lightbody that his Grandpa

On his third birthday Prince Charles paid a visit to his grandfather at Buckingham Palace.

Prince Charles playing a toy trumpet in the garden of Clarence House.

had gone away. This was very perplexing for the little boy, who could not understand why his Grandpa should have left without saying goodbye as he usually did. He asked to see his Granny and was told that he would have to wait. The Queen came to see him later.

Sitting her grandson on her knee, she told him that his Mother and Father would be home soon, much sooner than expected. Though this news was obviously welcome to the little boy, it only added to his confusion. Again he asked where his Grandpa had gone, and in spite of her self-control Queen Elizabeth burst into tears. She hugged her grandson to her, trying to disguise her grief, but when he patted her hand and said, 'Don't cry, Granny,' the others in the nursery could no longer hold back their tears.

The news of the King's death was made public at 10.45 a.m. An hour later one of the bells of St Paul's Cathedral began to toll solemnly once a minute for two hours. Black drapes were hung in shop windows, and the blinds of Buckingham Palace were drawn in mourning. At five o'clock in the afternoon, the Accession Council assembled in St James's Palace and declared Princess Elizabeth to be the new sovereign. Two hours later the Lords and Commons began to swear oaths of allegiance to their new Queen.

The news reached the Princess while she and Prince Philip were staying at a hunting-lodge which had been given to them by the people of Kenya as a wedding-present. A reporter on the *East African Standard* had telephoned the Princess's private secretary with the news. He in turn had rung Michael Parker at the royal residence, from a hotel across the valley. Parker tried to find confirmation of the report on the radio, but all he succeeded in picking up was solemn music being broadcast by the BBC. This was enough to convince him that the report was true. He walked round to the long living-room where the Edinburghs were sitting and signalled for the Duke to step outside without attracting the Princess's attention. When Prince Philip came out, Parker told him what had happened and then left him to break the news privately to his wife.

Placing her duty before her personal grief, Elizabeth directly set about tackling her first priorities as Queen. There were telegrams to be sent to the heads of state of the countries she would no longer be able to visit; she had to instruct the Privy Council to meet as soon as the Accession Council had declared her Queen, and she had to announce that she wished to be known by the name 'Elizabeth II', since she was free to choose whatever name she wished. As she sat working at her desk and for the first time signing documents 'Elizabeth R', her husband and Michael Parker were working out the fastest way back to London.

At half past four the following afternoon, 7 February, the Queen's aircraft came to a halt at Heathrow Airport, beside the line of bare-headed dignitaries waiting to greet their new monarch. Dressed in black, the pale, tense young woman of twenty-six cut a very tragic figure, arousing the sympathy of all her subjects as she descended the steps and was driven away to London.

As she drove up to Clarence House, she saw the upright figure of her grandmother waiting to greet her. When she stepped from the car, the Royal Banner was run up in her honour for the first time, and Queen Mary came forward to kiss her hand.

The silent, melancholy crowd that lined the Mall outside to catch sight of the new Queen was very different from the boisterous, jovial throng that had greeted her first son. And, though he did not realize it, Prince Charles's position was now very different too. By his mother's accession he was now Duke of Cornwall, Duke of Rothesay, Earl of Carrick, Baron Renfrew, Lord of the Isles, Great Steward of Scotland and Heir Apparent to the British throne. All this at only three years, two months and twenty-four days old.

2

The Duke of Cornwall

In spite of the changes in her own position, the new Queen was determined that there should be no sudden change in her children's lives. Indeed, to begin with, their daily routine went almost unaltered. The family still lived in Clarence House. There were still walks with one of the royal nannies and 'Jumbo', a fluffy blue elephant on wheels, with whose long-suffering assistance Charles had mastered the rudiments of walking. Perhaps most important of all there were still the regular visits to mother after breakfast and after tea.

The Queen decided to leave her children at Sandringham when the senior members of the family returned to London for her father's funeral. So Charles and Anne were spared the upsetting sight of the coffin and the solemn funeral cortège that bore their grandfather away from Buckingham Palace for the last time. However, there was one change in their lives which could not be disguised: after the funeral, when the family returned from a somewhat subdued Easter at Windsor (the Court was still in mourning), they drove to Buckingham Palace, not Clarence House.

Charles's grandmother and aunt Margaret had moved into his previous home, Clarence House, and the two children now found themselves living in new nursery quarters in the Palace, one floor above their parents' apartments which overlook Constitution Hill. In an effort to lessen the impact of this change, the new nursery had been decorated in the same colours as the old one. There were familiar objects too, such as Charles's toy-cupboard and his mock-Tudor dolls' house, so it did not take the children long to get used to their new domain. Here Charles drilled his regiments of toy soldiers, here he and his mother played with twenty-six wooden blocks on the carpet, learning the letters of the alphabet, and here he first displayed his artistic talents with crayons and paints.

For all her attempts to give Charles and Anne a normal upbringing, the Queen could not overlook the factors that would ultimately set them apart from other children. Unlike most children, they lived in a palace with over six hundred rooms. Unlike most children, Prince Charles had his own private detective and chauffeur. He and Anne had nannies and servants to look after them, and soldiers clad in magnificent scarlet uniforms marching up and down outside the front door.

OPPOSITE *A striking photograph of Prince Charles and Princess Anne taken by Antony Armstrong-Jones (later Lord Snowdon).*

This does not mean that they were cosseted or spoiled. On the contrary, both their parents were adamant that they should be made to value and appreciate the advantages that they enjoyed. The Queen and Prince were anxious too that their children's careful training for public service should begin right from the start. This training marked a significant departure from that previously administered to royal children and led to a relaxation of the strict formality and protocol that had characterized the royal households of the past.

Everyone within the Palace was instructed to call the children 'Charles' and 'Anne' and not 'Your Royal Highness', as had been the case with royal children in the past. Remembering how much her father had been upset whenever his two daughters had entered a room and curtsied to him as King, the Queen also did away with the old custom and spared her children this act of respect. However, she insisted they show due respect to their grandmother and great-grandmother in the old-fashioned way by bowing or curtsying to them whenever they paid a visit.

So the Palace that had once been described as a morgue by a former Prince of Wales, later Edward VII, was filled with the happy sounds of children playing. Charles used to dash along the miles of corridors pursued by the royal corgis and

later by a slower but equally determined younger sister. The upper floors of the Palace frequently resounded with the noise of the Heir Apparent beating time on an old saucepan with a wooden spoon, and whenever his father was left in charge, it was claimed that the sound of their bath-time could be heard throughout the Palace. There was only one room from which they were excluded, the Queen's private sitting-room that also served as her study. It is interesting that even this restriction was lifted to the two younger Princes, Andrew and Edward, and this has been taken by many as an indication of the Queen's greater ease and confidence in her constitutional rôle.

Like other young children, Charles and Anne were duly punished when they were naughty. In spite of letters from the public appealing to both nannies to spare the royal behinds, they were strong believers in the merits of a timely spanking. Prince Philip too is an advocate of discipline, not as a means of cowing or subduing childish spirits but to instil self-control and respect for others, especially in people who might easily be led to believe they could please themselves without any concern for others.

When Charles yielded to the temptation of popping an ice-cube down a

OPPOSITE *Prince Charles shows his mother a glove puppet during a summer holiday at Balmoral.*
LEFT *Looking very much the chubby toddler, Prince Charles experiments with a camera.*

THE DUKE OF CORNWALL

2 June 1953. Prince Charles arrives at Westminster Abbey with his nanny (right) to witness part of the Coronation of his mother Queen Elizabeth II. At four-and-a-half years old he was considered too young to take his place with the hereditary peers for the ceremony, but was allowed to watch part of the long service from the Queen Mother's box (below).

footman's neck, he was punished. When he stuck out his tongue at a crowd waving at him, his father spanked him soundly. The Queen was equally vigilant when it came to good behaviour. She was determined that the deference shown to him by others should not be allowed to turn his head. On one occasion, when he addressed one of her private detectives by his surname alone, as he had heard his parents do, the Queen ticked him off smartly and sent him back to apologize to the unfortunate officer. Once, while they were staying at Sandringham, she sent Charles off to search for a dog's lead he had lost in the grounds. Reminding him that dogs' leads cost money, she told him not to come back until he had found it.

With so many servants around them, it would have been easy for the royal children to become accustomed to being waited on hand and foot. Yet here again their parents were explicit that they should do things for themselves and not take the presence and services of others for granted. Once, when a footman hurried to close a door after Charles had come into a room to see his father, the Duke told the man to leave the door alone, saying that his son had hands and could perfectly well close it himself. Another incident occurred one Christmas at Sandringham when Prince Philip walked out of the house on a chilly winter morning to find the Heir Apparent bombarding a local policeman with snowballs. Charles's target was patiently suffering the attack, uncertain whether to return fire or ignore it, when he heard Prince Philip shouting to him: 'Don't just stand there, man. Throw some back.'

Unlike many royal children, who had been forced to endure harsher discipline in past ages, Charles and Anne never resented any of these admonitions. A telling-off from a mindful, loving parent was forgotten almost as soon as it was given, but the lesson was not.

Even as a little boy, Charles began to show signs of the consideration and thoughtfulness for others that were to endear him to millions around the world when he grew older. Whereas his more rumbustious sister, like her mother before her, relished walking backwards and forwards in front of the sentries, causing them to present arms each time she passed, Charles preferred to admire their scarlet tunics, flashing brass buttons and tall busbies at a respectful distance, no doubt to the intense relief of the guards on duty.

The young Prince took a concerned interest in his little sister's development. Even while she was still in a cot, he would press visitors to the Palace to come and see the baby. He also tried to pass on to her his own attention to good manners and polite behaviour. Leaving their carriage after a train journey, he would spontaneously lead Anne along the platform to the front of the train to thank the engine-driver.

With the many demands made upon her time in the fulfilment of her official duties, the Queen has jealously guarded the few periods of privacy that she spends with her family. In those early years, when the two children were still little more than babies, she tried to spend as much time with them as she could. On fine days they would have picnic teas in the gardens. The children would romp in the sand-pit or play on the swings, while the Queen sat on the grass in the sun enjoying a welcome

Saluting to the cheering crowds after a Trooping of the Colour Ceremony.

break from her desk. When their father joined them, there were more boisterous games of football, with the corgies joining in to add to the general confusion. During those early years too the Queen had asked the Prime Minister to put back his weekly visit on Tuesday evenings by one hour: the week's report on the proceedings in Parliament had to wait until after the children had been put to bed and read their bedtime story.

However, a conflict did arise between her joint rôle as mother and Queen during the preparations for the Coronation. One of the essential features of the Coronation service was the swearing of the oath of allegiance to the new sovereign by the Lords of State and Church. The full act of homage was to be performed by the royal dukes and the senior peers of the other grades, and in 1953 it was the Duke of Cornwall, aged four and a half, who headed the entire peerage. As this was the first occasion since the establishment of the dukedom in the fourteenth century that a sovereign was to come to the throne with so young a son, the decision whether Prince Charles should swear the oath of allegiance or not was left to the Sovereign, his mother.

The Duke of Cornwall had first appeared at a public entertainment two days after his fourth birthday. His mother and grandmother had taken him to the Royal Festival Hall to attend Sir Robert Mayer's Concert for Children. He had become visibly bored and restless half-way through and had had to be taken home before the concert ended. With this in mind, the Queen decided that it would be better for her son not to lead the other royal dukes and peers in the solemn Coronation oath-taking. It was decided instead that he should watch part of the proceedings from the royal box, under the watchful eyes of his aunt and grandmother.

As far as the children were concerned, the most interesting part of the Coronation was probably the period of extensive preparations that led up to it. The whole Palace was a hive of exciting activity. They took a great interest in the clothes their mother would be wearing when she entered and left Westminster Abbey (Charles was delighted to discover that the long cloaks his mother would be wearing were called 'trains'). From the nursery windows they could see the wooden stands being erected for the spectators along the Mall, while almost every day there were military bands or formations of soldiers marching outside in preparation for the great day. After watching one of these displays that seemed more significant than the others, Princess Anne rushed to tell Charles that the Coronation had started, only to be informed by her brother that what she had in fact seen was the Changing of the Guard. Up in the nursery the nannies and footmen were enlisted to play Coronations, while down in the mews Charles on one occasion had the thrill of riding in the Coronation coach.

On the morning of 2 June 1953, the children awoke to the sound of crowds of thousands of people gathering along the Mall and far away into the distance. There was the sound of bugles and the tramp of troops taking up their positions. When the mile-long procession finally got underway, the children watched it leave the Palace gates and slowly disappear into the distance towards Admiralty Arch. In the middle was the golden coach carrying their parents, with their mother dressed like a fairy-tale Queen, smiling and waving to the cheering crowds.

Once the procession had left, Charles was dressed in a white silk suit, his normally unruly hair was slicked down with hair-oil and he was taken down to the car which was to drive him to Westminster Abbey by another route. He entered the Abbey holding hands with his nanny and a Grenadier Guards officer and slipped into the front row of the royal box beside his aunt and grandmother.

The scene that confronted him must have been bewildering to a little boy of four. The Abbey was filled with the sound of the choir singing Handel's setting of the anthem 'Zadok The Priest'. His mother had been divested of her magnificent crimson robes and, wearing only the simplest white dress, she was sitting in the Coronation Chair. Around her stood four Knights of the Garter holding a canopy of cloth-of-gold above her head as the Archbishop of Canterbury prepared to anoint her with the consecrated oil. Sensing that her little son might be anxious at what was happening to his mother, the Queen was seen to glance towards the small white figure, and a slight smile of reassurance greeted the young Prince's worried gaze.

The thrilling spectacle of the splendid colours of the uniforms and costumes, the flashing of the religious plate and the sound of the anthems and hymns echoing in the high vaulted roof kept Charles enthralled. The Queen Mother was bombarded with questions throughout the ceremony, though she had to restrain him only once

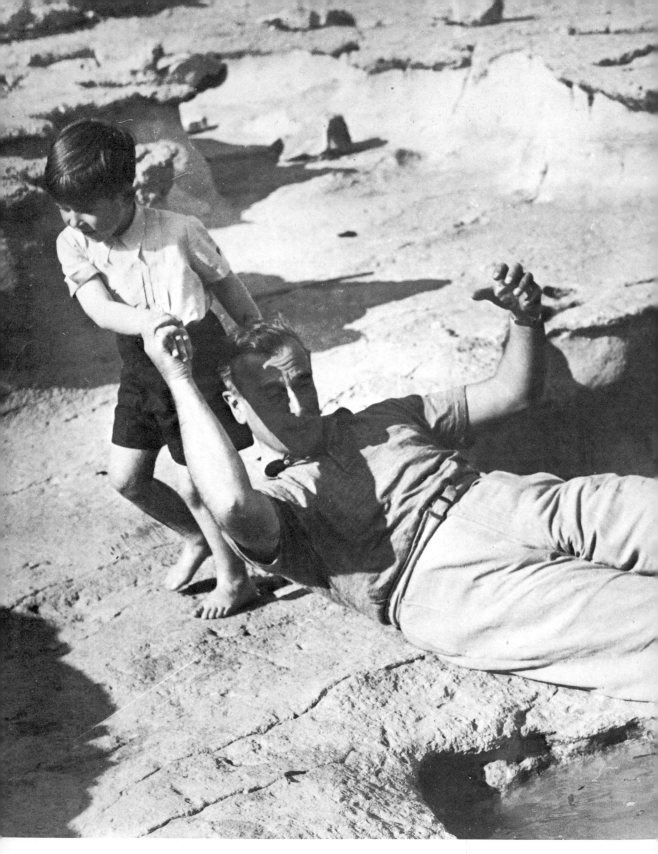

Charles and Anne made a short stop-over in Malta on their way to rejoin their parents after a Commonwealth tour (below). During his stay Prince Charles enjoyed a boisterous game with 'Uncle Dickie' (Lord Mountbatten).

From an early age Charles and Anne were trained to be polite and composed while in the public eye. Left Posing for a formal portrait and (right) Charles chats to the driver of the train he is about to board.

from leaning too far over the rail to have a closer look.

By the time the service had reached the point when the peers were to give their oaths of allegiance, Charles had already been allowed to stay longer than had originally been anticipated. But since it might have been constitutionally incorrect for him to observe the oath-taking, without actually taking part himself, Mrs Lightbody led him back to the car to be taken home for lunch.

When the service had finished, his parents rode home through the streets of the West End in order to wave to the thousands of people who had not been able to watch their procession to the Abbey. Like millions of others, Charles and Anne watched this on a newly installed television set. When their parents returned to the Palace, it was time for the children to appear on the screen themselves.

For a few moments the Queen stood alone on the balcony while her subjects shouted their congratulations and best wishes in an uproar of cheering. Then, holding their father by the hand, Charles and Anne were led out to join their mother.

For the first time in his life the little boy came face to face with mass adulation. He seemed remarkably self-possessed as, aged four, he began to come to terms with the deafening roar of the crowds and the thousands of smiling faces turned towards him. From then onwards he was to become more and more a centre of public attention himself.

Following the Coronation, however, photographs of the two children were carefully restricted, and they were seldom allowed to see those few that did appear in the papers. There had been criticisms that they had been given too much exposure in the Press, and the Queen was herself becoming worried about the adverse effect that this premature publicity might have on them.

Like most children in Britain, Charles began his official education at the age of five. Happily for him, this coincided with the start of the royal tour which would take both his parents away from home for six months. The royal tour of the Commonwealth which had been first postponed five years before, due to his grandfather's ill-health, was now scheduled to begin less than a fortnight after his fifth birthday. So, hoping that a new interest might help to distract his attention from their absence, his parents began preparations for his education and thereby introduced great changes to the Palace routine.

Though declining to follow advice from certain quarters that she should send her son to the local primary school, the Queen did break with tradition by appointing a governess to teach Charles, instead of the male tutors who had been employed in the past. This governess was Catherine Peebles – 'Mispy' to her royal charges. Recommended by Princess Marina, Duchess of Kent, whose children she had helped to educate, Glasgow-born Mispy arrived at the Palace and completed what became jokingly known in the royal household as 'the Scottish Mafia' in the nursery.

The Queen had considered inviting children from suitable backgrounds to join Charles in his lessons. However, it was decided it would be better for him to begin his lessons on his own, as he tended to be timid with other children and this might have hampered his educational development right from the start. Mispy quickly discovered that her pupil was more self-contained than most children of his age, that he was polite and responsible and that his sense of humour was very private.

While the Queen and Prince Philip were away, they kept in regular contact with their children by long-distance telephone calls and postcards from the places they had visited. Mispy used this as a useful way to introduce her pupil to geography and Charles quickly learned to trace his parents' route across the world on a globe.

Lessons in history began with the study of 'Children in History', in which Mispy traced the lives of famous historical figures right back to the time when they were Charles's age. It was with arithmetic however that Charles found the greatest difficulty and he was to struggle with the subject throughout his schooldays.

As the lessons with Mispy continued, Charles became gradually more confident and began to shed some of his shyness. As a result of his careful tuition, he was noticeably more self-assured by the time he was due to be reunited with his parents.

Eager to see Charles and Anne after the long period of separation, the Queen had arranged for them to join her and Prince Philip at the Libyan port of Tobruk. The new royal yacht *Britannia* had recently finished her sea trials, and it was decided that the children would sail to the Mediterranean with her.

When they drove to Portsmouth with their grandmother on the day the *Britannia* set sail, the Queen Mother was delighted to see that a sand-pit and slide had been installed on the upper deck, and a pedal-car had been converted into a miniature model of the ship for the children's amusement.

After an initial day of finding their sea-legs, and stomachs, they quickly settled into life aboard ship and thoroughly enjoyed the week's cruise to Malta. Charles ran around barefoot most of the time, helping the crew to scrub the decks and playing with them when they were off duty, while in the evenings there were special film-shows laid on to entertain the two royal children.

When they reached Malta, they spent a week with their great-uncle, Earl Mountbatten, who was then Commander-in-Chief of the Mediterranean Fleet. With him they explored the ancient fortifications of the island and the warm rock-pools of the coast. Charles had his first glimpse on board a warship when he accompanied Earl Mountbatten on an inspection of the aircraft-carrier HMS *Eagle*. After this short break, *Britannia* continued her voyage to meet the royal party at Tobruk.

One hundred and sixty-two days after she had last seen her children, the Queen was piped aboard the royal yacht. Seeing the officers and crew lined up to shake hands with her, Charles tried to join on the end to offer his hand to his mother. 'No, not you dear,' she was heard to say as she led her little son away to the state apartments for their long-awaited and very private reunion.

After the six months of separation the children had changed almost beyond their parents' recognition, and the remainder of the voyage must rank as one of the family's happiest memories. The King of Libya presented Charles with a magnificent Arab saddle and harness, and in Gibraltar the garrison presented the children with a model train-set of the Rock made out of papier-mâché. Though Charles was not normally as fond of mechanical toys as other little boys his age, he was absolutely thrilled with this unique souvenir, and he and Prince Philip spent many hours playing with it when they returned home.

In the course of his first year with Mispy, Charles quickly took to reading, although his skill with a pen was less advanced. His daily walks were replaced by educational visits, first to the landmarks familiar to all children who visit London for the first time, such as the Tower of London and Madame Tussaud's, but later to various museums in the capital.

However, as the pattern became more established, so the public interest in the Prince's excursions intensified, and more often than not the afternoon's educational

OPPOSITE *The Queen, the Queen Mother and a truculent Prince at an open air sports event.*

A royal party attends a sale of work organized by the Queen Mother to raise funds for the church at Crathie Castle, where the Royal Family worship while at Balmoral.

tour became a flight from reporters and cameramen.

This unwelcome development caused the Queen great anxiety. It seemed that her revolutionary decision to try to give her son a more liberal education stood in jeopardy. If he was to be pursued and hounded by the Press on these brief visits beyond the Palace railings, what chance was there of his being allowed to live a normal school life, if he ever went to school with other children? As an indication of her concern, she instructed her Press secretary, Richard Colville, to write to the editors of all the newspapers explaining her wishes. This was the letter they received:

I am commanded by the Queen to say that Her Majesty and the Duke of Edinburgh have decided that their son has reached the stage when he should take part in more grown-up educational pursuits with other children.

In consequence, a certain amount of the Duke of Cornwall's instruction will take place outside his home; for example, he will visit museums and other places of interest. The Queen trusts, therefore, that His Royal Highness will be able to enjoy this in the same way as other children without the embarrassment of constant publicity. In this respect, Her Majesty feels it equally important that those in charge of, or sharing in, the instruction should be spared undue publicity, which can so seriously interrupt their normal lives.

Prince Charles chases a runaway calf on the Balmoral Estate.

I would be grateful if you will communicate the above to your members and seek their co operation in this manner, informing them at the same time that they are at liberty to publish this letter if they so wish.

While on the one hand this appeal relieved the young Prince and his companions of their habitual posse of pressmen, on the other it gave rise to a host of fictitious reports, fabricated in order to answer the public's insatiable demand for news about the royal children. Since the Palace issues official denials only under very exceptional circumstances, most of these stories passed unchallenged. However, at least the orderly pattern of Charles's life was allowed to remain unaffected.

Lessons with Mispy were now broadened to include French, but Charles was still making hard work of his arithmetic. Nevertheless, by this stage in his life certain dominant passions were beginning to appear in other spheres. Mounted on a Welsh pony called William, he had started riding-lessons, although he was never to show the same rapid progress in the saddle as his sister. Under the instruction of his father and Michael Parker, Charles developed into a keen and proficient swimmer. His love of animals had extended beyond the Palace corgis, for the nursery was by then the home of a hamster named Chi-Chi, Charles's rabbit called Harvey and a pair of South American love-birds, David and Annie.

Watching their son's development as he approached his eighth birthday, the Queen and Prince Philip set about planning the next stage of his education – the transition from the royal nursery to the school classroom. A quarter of a century later it is difficult to appreciate the significance of the decision Her Majesty took in sending Charles away from the Palace to be educated alongside other boys of his own age, but at the time it marked a major change in the education of royal children.

The education of Edward VII, Edward VIII and George VI had been singularly inappropriate for the individuals in question. Queen Victoria's eldest son was subjected to a harsh routine of unrelenting study and discipline that had been tailored for him by his unbending father, the Prince Consort. As the boy had little aptitude for studying the strain of this regime became unbearable and he was frequently reduced to desperate fits of uncontrollable rage.

Two generations later, King George V's sons Edward VIII and George VI did not fare much better. Although George V had enjoyed good relations with his parents, he seemed incapable of establishing a similar relationship with his own children. He was frequently gruff and overbearing, and treated his children more as miscreant midshipmen than as his own offspring.

The boys' tutor, along with many others, advised the King that they would fare far better at a school where they could mix with others. However, George V was adamant that they could have no better education than his own, and this meant cloistered tuition at home followed by being pitched head first into the maelstrom of the Royal Naval College at Osborne, after which they both spent token periods at university. Such an education could hardly be construed as ideal for future kings of a leading twentieth-century industrial nation.

Deciding whether or not to send Charles to school was therefore not a straightforward matter for his parents. The attention aroused by his educational visits with Mispy had indicated the sort of public reaction there would be to the first heir to the throne in history attending an ordinary school. In spite of Colville's letter to the newspaper editors, the Queen could hardly expect the Press to ignore a good story for the whole of her son's school career.

In addition, she had to bear in mind the effect that mixing with other boys would have on the shy and introspective Prince. Her father had suffered miserably at Osborne, and she was not prepared to let the same fate afflict her son. However, Prince Philip was sure that the only way to overcome his shyness was for Charles to mix with other children in a purposeful, orderly environment.

After due consideration of the best way of introducing Charles to the idea of attending lessons with other boys, away from his nursery, the Queen invited the headmaster of a recently established boys' school to tea one afternoon, shortly after the beginning of the school year in 1956.

Several of the Queen's friends had recommended Henry Townend's pre-preparatory school, Hill House, to her, and over tea she asked Colonel Townend if he would accept her son as a pupil. Understandably flattered by this royal request,

The Queen was determined that Charles (right) should enjoy a more open education than his predecessors Prince Edward and Prince Albert, shown here with their tutor (left).

Colonel Townend was also not a little perturbed at the prospect of the responsibility.

Apart from being anxious about the welfare of the Heir Apparent in the rough and tumble of a school of 120 little boys, he was equally worried about the disruptive effect that the inevitable Press interest might have on the running of the school and on the lives of the staff and other pupils. However, Charles was hardly a pupil he could refuse to accept, so it was agreed that to minimize any problems he should start by merely attending the afternoon sessions on the playing-fields.

As before, Charles had his daily lessons with Mispy in the morning. After lunch he put on his school uniform and was driven to the school in Knightsbridge, where he changed into his games kit and joined the crocodile of other little boys walking two abreast across the King's Road to the Duke of York's Headquarters, where the school had use of playing-fields.

After the initial flurry of Press attention, the young Prince soon became indistinguishable from the other boys dressed in the school's uniform of rust-coloured blazer, shorts and cap. Besides, his own apparent lack of interest in the games soon led the Press interest in him to die away. Though Hill House could never be described as a typical school for boys of Charles's age, it was ideally suited to the needs of a young Prince. For one thing, most of the pupils came from the upper

echelons of diplomatic, government and service families. Many of them were the sons of foreign ambassadors and attachés stationed in London, which was a useful bonus for Charles, who in later life would be meeting people from all over the world.

Hill House aimed to mould its pupils in such a way that they would subsequently drive the maximum benefit from the orthodox public school system. However, it differed from conventional pre-preparatory schools in several respects: there was no corporal punishment; the boys were allowed free run of the confined school buildings, including the headmaster's dining-room. However, great emphasis was put on personal discipline, and the greatest crime a Hill House boy could commit was bringing disgrace on the school uniform. The syllabus too was broader than that normally available to boys of that age, and it even included classes in elementary anatomy taken by the headmaster's wife.

The Queen and Colonel Townend agreed that Charles should start attending the school properly at the beginning of the following term. Thanks to Mispy's careful instruction, a pre-school test showed that he was sufficiently advanced to start in form six, in the middle of the school.

Prince Philip was away in Australia and Antarctica during the preceding Christmas holidays. Michael Farebrother, the young headmaster of St Peter's School, Seaford, was invited to join the royal family at Sandringham as the Prince's 'tutor-companion'. No doubt it was hoped that the company of this schoolmaster would help to introduce the 'new boy' to the atmosphere of school life, in which most of his future teachers would be men. Nevertheless, when the day came for Charles to make history by becoming the first Heir Apparent to the British throne to go to school, he faced a monumental ordeal.

In spite of all his parents' careful preparations and their concern that his life should be as normal as possible, it was clear that he could never be just an ordinary schoolboy. With virtually no experience of the everyday lives of his classmates, he faced even greater difficulties than most new boys in conforming to type. He had never handled money. He had never queued in a sweet-shop to buy his own sweets. He had still not achieved his lifelong ambition of riding on a bus. But most important of all, he had never been left on his own before.

However, on 28 January 1957 pupil 102 ran up the steps of Hill House to be thrust into the mêlée of school life for the first time. Back at home that evening, he recounted the events of that important day to his anxious mother. As she listened to him cataloguing the lessons, the lunch of beef and carrots followed by apple pie, the game of basket-ball in the padded gym and the picture he had painted of Tower Bridge, the Queen must have felt a great sense of relief. Her experiment had, it seemed, got off to a good start.

OPPOSITE *Her Majesty with Prince Charles and Princess Anne plus two of the corgis, another photograph taken by Antony Armstrong-Jones.*

Prince Charles playing ball (left) *and dismantling a field gun* (right) *during the Hill House Field Day.*

The following morning her optimism waned. The Press had got wind of the Duke of Cornwall's latest activity. Together with a band of local residents, a gaggle of reporters and cameramen crowded the entrance to the school, waiting for him to arrive. When his car drew up, half an hour late, Charles had to run the gauntlet of camera-lenses and flashbulbs.

On the third morning the crowd was just as large, and when Colonel Townend telephoned the Palace to inform the Queen, it looked as if her bold experiment might have to be curtailed and Charles might have to be withdrawn once more behind the railings of Buckingham Palace to be taught by private tutors. Realizing the seriousness of the situation, the Queen's Press secretary, Richard Colville, went into action straight away.

Having identified the reporters besieging the school, Colville rang up each of their editors and reminded them of his earlier letter. The editors immediately called off their staff and Hill House was allowed to return to its normal routine, except for pupil 102, for Charles developed tonsilitis on the fourth day of term and was forced to stay at home for three weeks.

Once back at school, however, Charles quickly made up for lost time and the end of term was marked by something of a personal triumph for him. The annual 'Field Day' was an important date in the school calendar and was particularly important for Charles. He had persuaded the headmaster to include a display of dismantling and re-erecting a field-gun, similar to the one the school had seen on a recent visit to the Royal Tournament. Throughout the term Charles's class had devoted much time to constructing their wooden artillery piece and practising the difficult exercise. When the Field Day came, the boys carried out their display with as much determination and effort as the sailors they were copying.

There was one sailor in particular whom Charles hoped to emulate above all others, and his self-confidence must have received a great boost that afternoon when, in front of the whole school, he heard his father's stentorian voice bellowing across the field: 'Well done, Charles.'

The Queen's obvious relief and confidence in Charles's development was confirmed by his first end of term report. Although undistinguished it was perfectly satisfactory. He had settled well into the life of the school. He showed no sign of trying to 'pull rank' and was, if anything, more polite to the staff than the rest of the pupils. His report read as follows:

> Lent 1957, Upper VI
> Reading: very good indeed; good expression
> Writing: good, firm, clear, well formed
> Arithmetic: below form average; careful but slow, not very keen
> Scripture: shows keen interest
> Geography: good
> History: loves this subject
> French: shows promise
> Latin: made a fair start
> Art: good, and simply loves drawing and painting
> Singing: a sweet voice, especially in the lower register
> Football: enjoying the game
> Gymnastics: good

Like his first term, the second term at Hill House was interrupted by a bout of tonsilitis, though this time the offending tonsils were removed, and Charles was allowed to keep them in his nursery in a jar of preservative.

Apart from his introduction to cricket, a game he never greatly enjoyed, the summer term followed the same pattern as the one before, and when Charles came to leave at the end of the school year, in July, his final report read much the same as his first. He was credited with having slightly above-average intelligence, showed considerable artistic talent but was still very much a plodder at those classroom subjects tht he had always found difficult.

Hill House had served its purpose well. Charles had emerged in the summer considerably more self-confident than he had been the preceding autumn. This was made evident in August when he readily joined the crews on board his father's yachts *Bluebottle* and *Bloodhound* during the annual races at Cowes.

He was going to need all this confidence though, when he faced the next major change in his life. That autumn he was going to leave the comforts of home to face the rigours of life at prep school.

3

Away at School

Once she had embarked on the plan of sending her son to school, the Queen knew that there could be no turning back. No matter what problems Charles or his parents might encounter in the future, removing him from the stream of normal education to the placid backwaters of Palace tutors would be tantamount to admitting that her experiment had totally failed. Any such action would make her son's later life all the more difficult, besides setting a very unfortunate precedent for any royal schoolchildren in the future. Almost as soon as Charles had started at Hill House, her attention was directed to the next stage of his education.

During the course of her official visits around the country, the Queen contrived to visit a number of preparatory schools. Although these visits were ostensibly part of her everyday programme, it soon became evident that her motives and interests were more those of a prospective parent than a visiting VIP. The fact that she was the VIP supreme, however, made her choice far more difficult than that of other parents in her position.

The problems that had initially arisen at Hill House had to be borne in mind. It was vital that any school attended by Prince Charles should be far away from the prying eyes and ears of Fleet Street. At the same time she had to remember the training that would be required to equip her son as a future King. He would not be called upon to display great academic genius, but he would be expected to be able to master a general knowledge of a wide range of subjects, and in the course of his work he would have to absorb and digest a great deal of information.

Therefore, while preparatory schools do exactly what their name implies, prepare pupils for their next school, it was very important that Charles's school should offer as wide a range of activities as possible. The Queen, with no royal precedent to follow and no experience of school herself, was very much guided by her husband. In spite of Press speculation every time she visited one school or another, the final choice of Prince Philip's old school must have seemed the most likely from the start.

With its origins dating as far back as the reign of Charles I, Cheam School has considerable justification for calling itself the oldest preparatory school in England.

OPPOSITE 20 *January 1958. Prince Charles, carrying his own case, casts a lingering glance behind him as he returns to Cheam School after the Christmas holidays.*

Prince Philip had been sent to Cheam by his uncle, Lord Louis Mountbatten. He had enjoyed his time there and, like most fathers, was keen that his son should follow in his footsteps. The Queen was perfectly happy to accept this decision, and she led a family expedition down to the school, to inspect it for herself and to introduce her son to the two headmasters, Peter Beck and Mark Wheeler.

Situated in sixty-five acres of ground, the school offered the isolation from pressmen that the family were hoping to find. Nevertheless, it was decided that Charles's detective should accompany him to school and live in the grounds. It was also agreed that the headmasters would write to the other parents to explain that the presence of the Heir Apparent would not be allowed to interfere with the normal life of the school. The Queen wanted it made clear that Charles would receive exactly the same treatment as any other boy in the school.

Charles might well have wished that his mother had adopted a less egalitarian stance as he struggled to find his feet in the strange environment. His heart must have sunk when he first saw the dormitories. When the Queen tested the ancient wooden beds, constructed in the days when springs were the exception rather than the rule, she ruefully commented: 'Well, you won't be able to bounce on these.' Unheated and uncarpeted, the dormitories at Cheam must have seemed like prison cells to the boy accustomed to the comforts of the nursery in Buckingham Palace. But perhaps Charles's greatest fear was the prospect of having to share these spartan conditions with seven complete strangers.

When the dreaded day came, the family travelled together on the night train from Balmoral to London. The Queen and Prince Philip then drove their son the sixty-five miles from Buckingham Palace to Headley, where the school is situated.

The family was met by Mr Beck, to whom Charles rather sheepishly raised his cap. His few pieces of luggage were unloaded, and before he could really appreciate what was happening, it was time to say good-bye to his parents and watch their car disappearing down the drive away from the school. For the first time in his life he would have to fend for himself, without the reassurance of returning to the warmth and comfort of home in the evening. Now he would not see his parents again until the first visiting-weekend.

Charles spent the first few days just trying to become accustomed to the daily routine in this bewildering new world. The boys were woken at 7.15 a.m. by a duty master who exhorted them to 'rise and shine'. After washing and dressing, they were inspected by the matron, before going down to the school hall for the morning prayers and the ritual shaking of hands with one of the headmasters. The boys took it in turns to wait on the others at meal-times, carrying the food and plates from the kitchens to the long wooden tables at which they sat. The morning lessons ran from 9.00 a.m. until 1.00 p.m., with a break for a bun and a glass of milk half-way through. On Wednesdays and Saturdays there were half-holidays, but the afternoons of the other weekdays were occupied by games or art and handicraft. High tea was served at 6.00 p.m., and with the exception of Sunday, when there was

The newly created Prince of Wales returns to Cheam School with other pupils after a Sunday morning service.

a film, the boys were in bed by 7.00 p.m.

Charles was able to merge into the day-to-day running of the school without too much difficulty, but it was much harder for him to integrate with the other boys. Many of them were wary of making friends with him for fear of being accused of 'sucking up' to the Prince. On the other hand there were others who deliberately hung around him solely to raise their own status. This only increased his sense of alienation. The boys he would have liked to be friends with hung back at first, because of who he was, while the ones whom he liked least attached themselves to him for the same reason.

As he had no experience of forcing his way into groups of other boys, Charles tended to remain on the periphery of their activities, and this was inevitably interpreted by many of them as royal arrogance. In fact, one of his closest friends at Cheam was a pupil as unique as himself. This was Mary Beck, daughter of the headmaster, the only girl in the school.

It was his enjoyment of sweets that helped him to break the ice with the other boys. Not long after his arrival at Cheam, a totally fictitious story appeared in the Press that he had been forced to auction some of his personal belongings, because his parents kept him so short of pocket-money. This story made its way across the Atlantic and eventually came to the attention of the Association of Retail Confectioners of America, which was holding a conference in San Francisco. The conference immediately voted to send the Prince a 'Red Cross' parcel of their assorted products, and this shipment of sweets greatly helped Charles's acceptance among the other pupils, when its contents were distributed around the school.

After a while the other boys began to realize that in most ways Charles was really no different from them. He had great difficulty with mathematics, which at least showed that he was human. He was also able to give as good as he got in their daily rough and tumbles, and on one occasion he forced a larger boy into a bath full of cold water single-handed, after his victim had held his head under a cold tap.

There was, however, one external factor that did emphasize the difference between Charles and his fellows, in spite of his gradual incorporation into the school: the persistent interest shown in the schoolboy Prince by the world's Press. Reporters and cameramen were constantly lurking round the school in the hope of catching a glimpse of him. Anyone remotely connected with the school was asked about Prince Charles, and this led to unpleasant rumours that members of staff and even some of the boys were receiving bribes for leaking information about him. Although these rumours were never confirmed, they bred an uneasy spirit in the school. Suspicion and distrust began to infiltrate Cheam life, and the very situation that the Queen wished to avoid seemed to be imminent. It became clear that either the Prince or the Press would have to go.

Therefore Richard Colville called a meeting of all the newspaper editors at Buckingham Palace, during the Christmas holidays following Charles's first term. Colville invited Peter Beck to explain what effects the presence of their employees was having on the school. He then told them that, unless the school was left alone to do its job and the Prince was left alone to get on with his work, the Queen would be forced to give up her ideas of giving her son a normal, open education. The message sank in, and for the rest of his time at Cheam, Charles and the school were free from the surveillance of the British Press. It was left to foreign journalists to hide in the bushes and offer bribes to local shopkeepers.

With the gradual improvement in school life, Charles found that the afternoons had a lot more to offer than dull team-games. He had the chance to acquire practical skills such as carpentry and pottery. There were activities similar to scouting, which introduced him to woodcraft, outdoor cooking and the study of wildlife. These were things that the country-loving boy could wholeheartedly enjoy, and they greatly helped to develop his self-confidence during his first year. Though still shy by nature, he was more sure of his fellows, and when he was given a new cricket bat at the beginning of the summer term, he was as eager to show it to his friends as any other boy.

Perhaps it was unfortunate, therefore, from his point of view, that this moment of acceptance should have coincided with one of the most important announcements that was ever made concerning the future rôle which was so clearly to set him apart from his fellows.

The Commonwealth Games were to be held in Cardiff in 1958, and they were due

The Royal Children are taken for a ride in a speed boat. Later Prince Charles was allowed to drive the boat himself at over twenty miles per hour.

to be opened and presided over by the Queen. However, she was prevented from attending at the last minute by an attack of sinusitis, and her place had to be taken by Prince Philip. At the end of the Games it was announced that the Queen would make a recorded address instead.

Charles and a few of his friends were allowed to watch the closing ceremony on television in the headmaster's study. First they heard Prince Philip speaking. Then the recording of the Queen's speech was played to the crowds in the arena. She expressed her regret at having missed the tour of Wales that she was to have made and the visit to the Games afterwards. She had watched many of the events on television, she told the audience, and she praised the spirit of sportsmanship that she had witnessed. She continued: 'I want to take this opportunity of speaking to all Welsh people, not only in this arena but wherever they may be. The British Empire and Commonwealth Games in the capital, together with all the activities of the Festival of Wales, have made this a memorable year for the Principality.' Pausing slightly, she went on quietly, 'I have, therefore, decided to mark it further by an act which will, I hope, give as much pleasure to all Welshmen as it does me. I intend to create my son, Charles, Prince of Wales today. When he is grown up, I will present him to you at Caernarvon.' The television screen was filled with the sight and sound of drumming applause and thirty thousand Welsh voices singing 'God Bless The Prince of Wales'. In the headmaster's study the response was equally jubilant. Charles's friends turned towards him, clapping and cheering, but the headmaster, who had been forewarned and was watching the Prince's reaction intently, saw only a look of acute embarrassment on his face. Instead of being able to submerge himself in the relative anonymity of the school, here he was being elevated to the position of second in rank in the most noble Order of the Garter, the oldest secular order of chivalry in Europe, and he was, by tradition, automatically created Earl of Chester as well. For the nine-year-old Prince this was very much a case of having greatness thrust upon him.

He had an opportunity to come to terms with these new honours during the summer holidays, and in his own perspective they were probably eclipsed by the prospect of no longer being a new boy when he returned to Cheam.

Charles was able to settle down to the next four years of his life much like any other schoolboy. In his class work he was again attributed with a higher than average intelligence, even though he attained only average results. His teachers realized that he had a far more extensive general knowledge than most boys of his age, while his use of English was also considerably more advanced. His one major drawback was his continuing inability to understand mathematics. Speaking of this in later life, Charles freely admitted his dislike of the subject: 'Maths taken in its pure context is a misery, I think. I find it boring. I'm one of those people who prefer ideas rather than numbers.'

Outside the classroom Charles started to take piano lessons and continued his singing, which he had begun at Hill House, by joining the school choir and singing in the local church, St Peter's, Headley. He built a sturdy wooden table in his carpentry classes, which he presented to his sister, who proudly displayed it in her room. His creative genius also inspired a grim work of art called 'Gallows and Stocks', which was commended in the Under-10 modelling exhibition.

As he made his way through the school, he grew to be more and more at ease with the other boys. His parents were careful that any gift he had at school should not be ostentatiously the largest or most expensive, and for his own part, Charles was always generous with his toys.

His thoughtful consideration for others was even extended to the games fields and the thick of a rugby maul, after which Charles could often be overheard apologizing to other players whom he had previously been trampling in the ruck.

A further indication of his increasing self-confidence was his willingness to take part in the school plays. At Cheam, only the top three forms were eligible for

OPPOSITE *An informal shot of the Prince at the annual Badminton three-day horse trials in Gloucestershire. This is one of the sports events at which the Royal Family is present every year.*

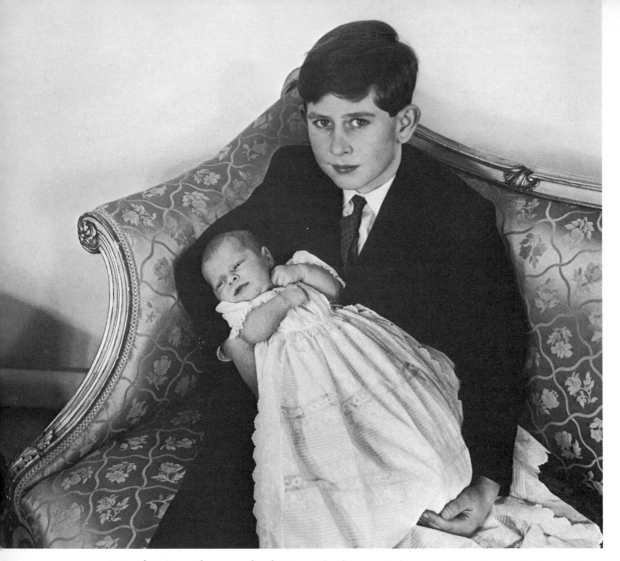

A Cecil Beaton photograph of Prince Charles, aged eleven, holding the newly born Prince Andrew in the blue porphyry drawing room at Buckingham Palace.

casting, which meant that Charles was half-way through his time at the school before he first took to the boards. An understudy's dream came true for him, when the boy who had been cast to play the main rôle in *Richard III* was unable to appear at the last minute, and Charles was called upon to take over the part.

To the delight and occasional amusement of the audience, the heir to the throne delivered lines on kingship that would have been perfectly innocuous in the mouth of any other actor. 'And may I soon ascend the throne,' said the Prince of Wales, with suitable gravity, though luckily the reigning Sovereign was not present to hear the dark threat. In fact the Queen's absence was explained during the performance, when the headmaster interrupted the play to announce that she had just given birth to a second son, a younger brother for Prince Charles, named Andrew.

This was a great thrill for Charles, who was predominantly a home-loving boy. He took a great interest in his baby brother just as he had in his sister eight years before. Now that he was older, Charles was able to bath the baby himself and take a more active part generally in bringing up his younger brother.

While he was at school, though, he never took more time off to be at home than any of the other boys, in spite of the temptation the Queen must often have felt to call him home for a number of royal functions. Like other mothers she visited him only three times a term. His father dropped in more frequently, and he was occasionally visited by his grandmother. Whenever the Queen and Prince Philip visited the school, they did so on the strict understanding that they were to be treated as ordinary parents. No special arrangements were to be made for them, and the Queen's only request was that no one should use a camera while they were there. So it was not uncommon for other parents walking in the grounds to come across a royal picnic, or for members of staff, going to investigate the cause of an unusual amount of noise in the gym, to find the Queen and her son playing excitedly on the apparatus there. Anne always competed in the visitors' race in the annual school sports, although she was never placed at the finish. But that was of little consequence to her brother, whose own athletic prowess left something to be desired.

Like many other boys forced to participate in team-games, Charles tolerated cricket and eventually graduated to the school's first XI, but he never enjoyed the game. Rugby on the other hand was a ceaseless succession of scrummages for Charles, who once complained bitterly that he was always made to play in the second row, the worst place in the scrum in his opinion. Probably the only team-game he ever remotely enjoyed was soccer, which he had played at Hill House. In fact, during his last year at Cheam, Charles captained the school's first XI during an unspectacular season in which they managed to lose every match.

While his skills on the playing field showed little sign of improvement, he was making rapid advances in field-sports during the holidays. This was thanks mainly to his father's encouragement and tuition. Charles shot his first grouse when he was ten, and by the time he left Cheam he was contributing respectable numbers to the Sandringham game-book. Fishing became another growing passion, and as Charles entered his teens he was to spend more and more time sharing this pastime with his grandmother, the Queen Mother, who was the family's number-one angler.

As Charles grew away from the influence of governesses and nannies and grew closer to his father, they spent far more time together. Prince Philip taught Charles to drive a car, and he was frequently seen driving a Land-Rover along the private roads of the family estates even before his thirteenth birthday. The landlady of the Pleasure Boat Inn, at Hickling, once found herself taking in two unexpected royal residents during the annual coot-shoot on the Broads. The Duke and Prince Charles had intended staying in a bungalow belonging to the Norfolk Naturalists Trust, but when they arrived they found it flooded and went along to the pub to ask for a bed. The lady of the house rose to the occasion with admirable calm and coped with the emergency by merely asking a friend, Mrs Mudd, to come and lend a hand. Mrs

Mudd, she informed her guests, helped her out when she was busy.

The other principal interest to which Prince Philip introduced his son at that time was polo. Although Charles did not take up the game until he was much older, he used to jump at the opportunity of watching his father playing, and Prince Philip would frequently give his son instruction on the practice-fields when he was not playing himself.

Perhaps the best guide to Charles's development was the growing confidence his parents placed in him. When he was convalescing after having his appendix removed in the spring of 1962, his mother asked him to attend one of her luncheon-parties in place of his father, who was abroad at the time. Whereas the timid schoolboy who had entered Cheam four years earlier would have quaked at the idea, Charles was by then able to chat freely with guests as varied as a trade-union leader, a choreographer, an industrialist and the chairman of the BBC. His status was rising at school too, where he had been made a monitor.

It had been a long, difficult transition from the Palace nursery to life at boarding-school, and it must have seemed to Charles that almost on the very day he at last became reconciled to his new life he was plucked away from it. This time he was to be incarcerated in an even harsher environment, one which, as far as Charles was concerned, probably sounded as if it was half-way to the Arctic Circle.

Up until his thirteenth birthday, Charles's education had been geared to preparing him for his secondary education, and in many ways the choice of his public school was the most important one his parents would make. The next five years had to be very carefully managed since they might be the last chance to give the Prince a formal education. As at Cheam, the Queen and Prince Philip were looking for a balanced, wide-ranging education that would equip Charles for the unique job that lay ahead of him.

Many people thought that the obvious choice of public school was Eton. The College was very near the Prince's home, lying just across the river from Windsor Castle. Charles's cousins Prince William and Prince Richard of Gloucester had both been educated there, and the school offered a wide range of activities, while catering for boys of very different academic abilities.

However, there were several factors that ruled out Eton in Charles's case. There were many critics who complained that the school was unrepresentative. Its élitist nature would, they claimed, prohibit the Prince from mixing with ordinary people in later life. There were even more cogent arguments put forward against Eton by the Royal Family itself. It was far too near Fleet Street and perhaps, in Prince Philip's mind, far too near the seductive comforts of home. Even though Charles had come a long way in developing his self-confidence, his father was still concerned that he lacked the drive and leadership that would be so necessary to a head of state in the twenty-first century.

The school chosen to mould the Prince for this exacting task had to bring out those qualities in him, or rather they had to provide the environment in which

1 May 1962. Prince Charles shakes hands with Gordonstoun's headmaster Robert Chew, on his arrival with his father to begin at his new school.

Charles could be made to discover those qualities in himself. There was no question in Prince Philip's mind. Only one school could serve this purpose, and that was his old school, Gordonstoun.

Charles was consulted by his parents throughout the period of decision-making. He had shown a slight preference for Charterhouse since many of his friends from Cheam were heading there, but he was content to be guided by his father, who had, he knew, been very happy at Gordonstoun. He must have had many private misgivings afterwards as he learned more about the school.

Gordonstoun was modelled on a German school that had been created by Prince Max Baden at his family home in Salem, in southern Germany, in 1919. Prince Max had witnessed the appalling collapse of Germany after the First World War, and he was determined that he would create a school in which national leaders could be educated to avoid such disasters in the future. The headmaster appointed by Prince Max to run the school was an educationalist named Kurt Hahn. Before the war he had studied at Oxford, as a Rhodes scholar, and had been favourably impressed by the English public-school system. In the aftermath of the German defeat he sought to instil similar ideals into his school, grafting what he saw as the best of English education onto the solid trunk of German aristocratic tradition. The result would, he hoped, be a system that would 'train soldiers who, at the same time, are lovers of peace'. However, as a Jew, and moreover as a Jew who vehemently criticized Hitler and the rising Nazi Party, he was forced to leave Germany in 1933 and not unnaturally came to Britain. With the assistance of certain influential friends, he acquired the lease of a seventeenth-century house set in three hundred acres of land in Morayshire, in Scotland, where in 1934 he opened a new school based on the same principles as the school he had been forced to leave in Salem.

In order to counteract the hours spent in the classroom, great emphasis was put on service to others in the community and on physical activities and attainments. Hahn wanted the pupils of Gordonstoun to follow the traditions of the monks who had originally occupied the castle at Salem when it was a monastery. He wanted them to develop an instinctive sense of charity, while also pitting themselves against physical challenges – mountains, the sea and the weather, to develop inner resources of determination, self-control and courage. The school motto, '*Plus est en vous*' ('There is more in you'), was chosen to emphasize the spirit of adventure and self-analysis that it was hoped all pupils would enter into. Charles can be forgiven, therefore, for his initial reaction that the place sounded 'pretty gruesome'.

His first visit to the school can have done nothing to reassure him. Life at Gordonstoun was even more spartan than life at Cheam. The dormitories consisted of single-storey huts. There was no paint on the walls, the floors were bare, and unshaded light-bulbs hung from the ceilings. The boys wore short trousers and took cold showers twice a day. All in all, Gordonstoun must have presented an appalling prospect to a boy who had taken four years to come to terms with the relatively civilized life at Cheam.

On the first day of the summer term Charles flew with his father to an airfield in Scotland and then continued the journey to Gordonstoun by car. The new gravel on the drive and the official welcome accorded to the royal visit were intended to honour Prince Philip, the distinguished old boy of the school; the new arrival had yet to prove his worth. After meeting Mr Robert Chew, the headmaster, who had been one of the original staff working with Kurt Hahn, Charles was allowed to have a final lunch with his father before Prince Philip left to collect his plane. As he flew south once more, he passed over his old school and dipped his wings as a passing salute to its newest pupil, who must have felt very lonely when he saw the plane disappearing into the distance.

Once again Charles found himself at the bottom of the school ladder. He was now reduced to the lowest level of the Gordonstoun hierarchy and was even distinguished as a new boy by having to wear a special blue uniform. The first rung of the ladder was the privilege of wearing the regular school uniform.

Whereas Cheam had been about the same size as Hill House, Charles was now pitched into a community four times larger than the one he had left and in which many of the pupils were indistinguishable from the staff, except for the short trousers the boys wore. For the first time too Charles came up against the aggressive antagonism of adolescents which had replaced the childish prep-school jibes of Cheam. He had the slight advantage of knowing three other boys in the school, Earl Mountbatten's grandson Norton Knatchbull and his cousins Prince Guelf of Hanover and Prince Alexander of Yugoslavia. Even these three were frequently taunted and mocked for showing any signs of friendship towards Charles.

On entering the school, he was made a member of Windmill Lodge, a stone and timber building situated about a quarter of a mile from Gordonstoun House. Charles shared the lodge with fifty-nine other boys. Their accommodation consisted of a bathroom with six showers and a bath, a locker-room, where the boys kept their clothes, and the dormitories where they slept on unyielding hair mattresses and wooden beds. They ate their meals in the main house, where most of the lessons were held and where the boys had room to do their private study.

The day at Gordonstoun began at 7 a.m. with the 'waker' rousing the others for a run round the grounds in shorts and vest before they returned to the Lodge for the first of the day's cold showers. They then made their beds and cleaned their shoes before going to the main building for breakfast.

Prince Charles about to mount his pony for a match at Guards Polo Ground, Windsor. Polo is one of the few team sports enjoyed by the Prince who prefers the personal challenges of solo sports.

The routine for the rest of the day was outlined in this official summary:

8.15 Breakfast. Surgery as necessary.

8.55 Morning Prayers.

9.10 Classwork begins. There are five forty-minute periods in the morning, but for every boy one of these, on several days of the week, is a training-break (running, jumping, discus- and javelin-throwing, assault course etc) under the Physical Training Master.

1.20 Lunch. After lunch there is a rest period (twenty minutes): music or reading aloud to boys relaxing on their backs.

2.30 Afternoon activities. On three days a week there are either games (rugger and hockey in winter, cricket, lawn tennis or athletics in summer), seamanship, or practical work on the estate. The proportion of time spent on each depends on a boy's interests and development. One afternoon a week is allocated to the Services: Coast Guard Watchers, Sea Cadets, Army Cadets, Scouts, Fire Service, Mountain Rescue and Surf Life-Saving. One afternoon and evening a week are given to work on boys' individual projects which are exhibited and judged at the end of each year. On Saturday afternoons there are matches and opportunities for expeditions.

4.00 Warm wash and cold shower. Change into evening school uniform. Tea. After tea, classes or tutorial periods.

6.20 Supper, followed by preparation in Houses or by 'Societies'.

9.15 Bedtime; silence period of five minutes.

9.30 Lights out. (There are some modifications for juniors.)

On those occasions when the boys were not engaged in some form of school activity, they were free to explore the surrounding countryside, although the town of Elgin was out of bounds. As at Cheam, Charles preferred these country rambles to the more orthodox alternatives. He made friends with many of the people living in the area and often spent afternoons with them walking, or shooting sometimes at the weekends. His indifference to team-games was not frowned upon at Gordonstoun as it might have been at many other schools. Far greater store was set by physical achievements or personal endeavour, and in this the sea was regarded as a very important training-ground.

Charles had already advanced beyond the lessons in elementary seamanship, thanks to his previous sailing experience. His swimming held him in good stead too, and he formed a life-saving partnership with his cousin Guelf which won them both their certificate of proficiency.

He found another test at sea even more demanding. He took part one day in a canoeing expedition which was planned to paddle to a point twelve miles along the coast. Shortly after they had set out, Charles's party were caught in a storm against which they battled all day long. By the time they returned home in the evening, they had covered well over the scheduled twenty-four miles and were all completely exhausted. One of Charles's few regrets about Gordonstoun was that he never had an opportunity to repeat the trip.

In the course of his first term Charles did more than his fair share of community

Now a very proficient skier, Charles first learned to ski in 1963, although lessons were hampered by the attentions of the Press.

work, heaving around the school's dustbins. But this, and his general performance during the term, entitled him to graduate to the status of wearing the school uniform by the end of term. The honour was accompanied by a traditional rite of a ducking, fully clothed, in a bath of cold water.

The modest success of this achievement and his academic report, which placed him near the top of the class, were obviously encouraging. Nevertheless, the first two terms at Gordonstoun were among the most wretched months of his life. He used to visit his grandmother at Balmoral to confide in her the misery and loneliness that dogged him continually. For all her commiseration and sympathy, however, the Queen Mother must have known that there was little that could be done to smooth her grandson's path. She knew that he would have to face the ordeal himself so that, when he finally won through, the success would be his alone.

Yet another trial was added to Charles's catalogue of misfortunes during the following Christmas holidays. He went to spend a short winter-sports holiday with his relations in Bavaria, but what had been intended as an enjoyable skiing break was turned into an unseemly stampede across the piste as the European Press floundered around the Prince, trying to record his every slip and tentative slide. In the end his lessons had to be given in the grounds of the castle where he was staying.

A year after arriving at Gordonstoun Charles was promoted to the Junior Training Plan and so rose to the next rung of the ladder. This entitled him to greater freedom and a wider choice of extramural activities. One that he chose was a cruise aboard the school yacht *Pinta*, on which, on 17 June 1963, he sailed into the harbour of Stornaway, on the Isle of Lewis, and into the world's headlines.

After making the yacht fast, Charles and four of the other crew-members were allowed ashore at lunchtime and given permission to go to the cinema in the afternoon. As usual they were accompanied by Charles's detective, on this occasion a Mr Donald Green. After leaving the boys in the Crown Hotel, Green went off to the cinema to arrange seats for the matinée performance. In the meantime word spread among the residents of Stornaway that the Prince of Wales was in the hotel, and a crowd began to gather outside the windows, peering in at the boys. Feeling acutely embarrassed in front of his school-friends and annoyed at being treated as a peep-show, Charles got up and went into the next room to get away from the sea of faces at the lounge window.

However, the next room was a bar where there were adults sitting and drinking. It was obvious that he was going to arouse even more attention unless he did something quickly. Although he was fully aware that it was against the law for a fourteen-year-old boy to drink in a bar, Charles may well have heard from other Gordonstoun boys that they had occasionally enjoyed a clandestine drink on these trips to Stornaway where everyone had turned a blind eye.

Whatever his motive, he ordered a cherry brandy, a drink he had sipped to keep out the cold while shooting. He paid his half-crown and sat down. At that moment a freelance journalist walked into the bar, recognized the guilty schoolboy drinking alcohol in the corner and seized upon the sensational scoop.

Within twenty-four hours 'the cherry-brandy affair' was news around the world.

30 July 1963. Prince Charles arrives back at Heathrow airport from school in Scotland. His slightly disconsolate expression may be due to the fact that he was still being criticized over the famous 'cherry-brandy incident' which had happened the month before.

Unfortunately for Charles it followed a series of censures he had received in the Press during the past few months. He had been criticized for shooting his first stag in the previous autumn and had been castigated that winter for skiing on a Sunday. Now teetotallers throughout the land were up in arms, and their reaction led the foreign Press to surmise that the Prince had been discovered indulging in some debauched bacchanal.

The incident was further aggravated by an official denial issued from the Palace, which had later to be withdrawn when it was disclosed that there had been a misunderstanding over a telephone conversation with Donald Green. As a result the incident received far more Press-coverage than it merited.

Charles had to face more than the hue and cry raised in the Press. He had to receive punishment from the school, whose reputation and trust in him had been tarnished by the affair. The headmaster decided to remove his recently acquired status in the Junior Training Plan instead of administering the cane, which Charles would have greatly preferred to being reduced to the ranks once again.

Although he quickly won back his place in the Junior Training Plan, the embarrassment and injustice of the incident still rankled, and the disproportionate coverage given to the incident unsettled him for some time. His feelings towards the Press were not warmed either by their eagerness to arraign him before the world at large. When Donald Green announced his resignation not long afterwards, Charles must have felt himself entirely to blame.

The following school year ended with an important test for all of Charles's form, their O-level examinations. As the first Heir Apparent ever to sit a public examination, he knew that he had to prove to himself and to his critics that he was capable of competing on an equal footing with any other candidate.

It was an important year for him in other respects. After 'the cherry-brandy incident' he had to regain confidence in himself and win back the confidence of others in him – both of which he succeeded in doing quickly by taking a more prominent part in the life of the School. It was during that year too that he went on his first archaeological dig, in Morayshire, and spent his first weeks with the Royal Navy, activities which were to play a large part in his later life.

In the end his O-levels were successful, though not dazzlingly so. He succeeded in passing in five subjects, those in which he was most competent: Latin, French, History and English Language and Literature. However, he failed Mathematics and Physics, and while the latter was hastily dropped, it took him another eighteen months to satisfy the examiners that he was worthy of a pass in his old adversary.

Once the results were published, Charles was able to enjoy the summer holiday with a feeling of relief and mild satisfaction. After the normal round of Balmoral and Cowes week there was an added treat in September, when Charles and Anne flew with their father to Athens, to attend the wedding of King Constantine of Greece to the Danish Princess Anne-Marie. Anne was to be the junior bridesmaid, and Charles was to be one of ten young men who were to take it in turn to hold gold

crowns above the heads of the bride and groom as required in the Greek Orthodox wedding service.

As Charles was standing holding the crown above the King's head during the ceremony, he began to realize the need to share the task. In spite of all his efforts to ignore the muscles aching in his outstretched arm, the crown began to waver ominously, and the Queen Mother, Frederika, had to come to his aid before the crown fell.

The wedding visit was also memorable for Charles as the occasion when he was able to exact some vengeance on the world's Press. While he was sunbathing with his sister and some of the other young royals on a raft floating off the beach at Vouliagmeni, a resort near Athens, three French photographers managed to slip through the cordon of Greek police patrolling in paddle boats to keep prying eyes at bay, and approached the royal raft. Someone on the raft noticed them, and in the ensuing fracas two of the photographers were pitched into the sea. Whether Charles was responsible for their ducking or not, he had plenty of reasons for enjoying it, especially as neither photographer came to any harm and they did succeed in printing their saturated pictures after all.

The new term had scarcely begun at Gordonstoun when it was announced that one of his exercise-books was missing, the one in which he wrote his weekly essays. It was clear that the book had been stolen, and when the headmaster informed the police, he impressed on them the value of such a book to a collector of royal memorabilia. In the end his fears were proved well founded, for the stolen book was soon being offered to newspapers and Press agencies at home and abroad. Six weeks after it first went missing, it was seized by police in Lancashire. However, this merely confirmed that the photostat copy in the possession of the German magazine *Der Stern* was in fact genuine. *Der Stern* set their translators to work, and three days after Charles's sixteenth birthday his weekly essays were published in German under the sensational title 'Confessions of Prince Charles'.

The 'confessions' actually consisted of essays on topics such as 'The Press, wireless and television services' and 'What four things I would take with me in the event of a nuclear emergency and evacuation to a place of safety'. All they revealed to the somewhat disappointed German readers was that Prince Charles appeared to be reasonably mature in his thinking, had a good command of the English language and was able to argue his point of view quite lucidly.

As it was, the publishing of the essays was aggravating enough, but what really sparked off the controversy was a further embellishment to the article, which prompted the infuriated staff of the royal household to issue another of their very rare denials. At the end of the article in *Der Stern* it had been intimated that Charles

OPPOSITE *At a Garden Party for Scottish youth in the grounds of Holyrood House Palace, the Royal Family's official Scottish residence, Prince Charles joins his parents for his first official engagement.*

Prince Charles in the title role of Macbeth, *in a Gordonstoun production. The play supposedly takes place in Glamis castle, which is the home of his grandmother's family the Bowes-Lyons.*

had deliberately sold the exercise-book to a friend for thirty shillings in order to augment his inadequate pocket-money.

This outrageous allegation led the American magazine *Time* to follow up with an article which claimed that Charles had been in the habit of selling his autograph to other boys while he was at Cheam. Once again Richard Colville came to the Prince's aid and answered the *Time* article 'The Princely Pauper' thus:

There is no truth whatever in the story that Prince Charles has sold his autograph at any time. There is also no truth whatever that he sold his composition-book to a classmate. In the first place he is intelligent and old enough to realize how embarrassing this would turn out to be, and second he is only too conscious of the interest of the Press in anything to do with himself and his family. The suggestion that his parents keep him so short of money that he has to find other means to raise it is also a complete invention. Finally, the police would not have attempted to regain the composition-book unless they were quite satisfied that it had been obtained illegally.

In spite of this denial, the affair rumbled on throughout the term and even into the Christmas holidays, part of which Charles and Anne spent skiing in Liechtenstein. On this occasion, though, the royal party came to an agreement with the Press: they would be allowed to photograph the young royals in the afternoons, provided that they left them in peace to enjoy their holidays during the mornings.

1965 saw the more frequent emergence of the Prince of Wales in public. In January he joined his parents at the funeral of Sir Winston Churchill. In the Easter holidays he attended his first meeting of the eight-man committee that looked after the Duchy of Cornwall. In June he accompanied his parents in his first major public engagement, a garden-party for Scottish and Commonwealth students which the Queen held at Holyrood House Palace. Charles was a great success with the guests and endeared himself to them all the more when he became carried away in one conversation and stayed talking for three minutes after his parents had moved off. He had to dash across the grass after them, catching up only seconds before the National Anthem ended the reception.

His last full year at Gordonstoun was marked by a number of personal successes. He played the trumpet in the school orchestra in several public concerts; he had been promoted to the position of Colour-Bearer (prefect); he had eventually passed O-level maths, and at the end of the Christmas term he had achieved his greatest acting success to date, the title-rôle in Shakespeare's *Macbeth*, a play in which his father had been cast as only a minor character, Donalbain.

Although these achievements contributed greatly to making life at Gordonstoun more bearable, Charles could not disguise the fact that he was becoming fundamentally bored with school and dearly longed for a change. He knew that, if he wanted to go on to university, he would have to complete his A-level studies at Gordonstoun. For the time being though, he wanted a break, and his parents, acknowledging that it would be a good thing for him to experience a different environment for a few months, agreed to his request.

On her Coronation visit to Australia the Queen had promised to send her son to that continent when he was older. Prince Philip too had liked what he had seen of the country during his service in the Royal Navy and the royal visits he had made there. So, when a Commonwealth school was suggested as a possible environment for Prince Charles during his time away from Gordonstoun, a school in Australia seemed to be a happy solution.

Sir Robert Menzies, the Australian Prime Minister at the time, was conveniently in London on a visit, and he was duly consulted on the most suitable school for Charles to attend. The selection fell on Geelong Church of England Grammar School, the so-called 'Eton of Australia'. Instead of sending Charles to the main body of the school in Melbourne, it was felt that he would enjoy himself far more if he went to Geelong's outward-bound colony on the slopes of Mount Timbertop, two hundred miles to the north.

Each year the school sent about 135 boys from the middle years to its mountain retreat. There they lived the rugged life of the outback, catering and fending for themselves. There was only a minimum of school work and school routine. In their place the boys were encouraged to develop their own powers of self-reliance and self-sufficiency. They had to cut their own firewood, raise their own livestock and generally maintain their own homestead throughout the year. In return the colony

offered unlimited opportunities for exploring and hiking. There was fishing available in the many streams that flowed through the gum-forests in which Timbertop was situated and all manner of wild life living in the thick undergrowth at the base of the tall trees. Although Timbertop must have sounded horribly reminiscent of Gordonstoun at first, Charles was to find it very different.

Nevertheless, when he flew out of London Airport in January 1966, he probably felt as isolated as he had when embarking on new lives at Cheam and Gordonstoun. Of course he did not travel entirely alone: he was accompanied by his detective and by Prince Philip's equerry, Squadron-Leader David Checketts, who was to act as mediator between the Australian government and the Prince. Checketts had the further unenviable task of trying to keep the Press well informed, while keeping them well away from the Prince.

Charles knew of the Australians only by reputation, as coarse and critical of 'pommies'. He was fully prepared for a rather lukewarm, even hostile, reception on his arrival, and when he first landed he was certainly greeted with an element of caution. After the usual official receptions he spent a couple of days relaxing in and around Canberra before being driven to Timbertop on 3 February.

Since Charles was a couple of years older than most of the other boys, he was looked upon as one of the leaders right from the start. Instead of sleeping in the dormitories, he was entitled to share a room in the master's quarters with a pupil from Geelong who was his own age. This senior boy, Stuart Macgregor, had come up to Timbertop to study for his university entrance exams, which made him an ideal companion for Charles, who had also to study hard for his A-levels in history and French the following summer.

Although David Checketts was responsible for the Prince's public relations work while he was in Australia, he did not live at Timbertop. He chose to rent a farm about 120 miles away which soon became Charles's Press headquarters as well as occasional weekend retreat, when he lived with the Checketts as a surrogate elder son and 'mucked in' with them as one of the family.

Part of the arrangement with the Press was that they would be allowed to follow Charles around on his first day at Timbertop, taking as many photographs as they wished. This was permitted on the understanding that they were then to leave him completely undisturbed, receiving all their information through David Checketts. It must have come as a pleasing surprise to Charles when the Australian Press kept to this agreement wholeheartedly. It was certainly one of the factors that greatly enhanced his enjoyment of life at Timbertop.

In the greater freedom of Australia Charles carried his title and rank far more easily than he had at school in Britain. He willingly joined in the hikes and arduous cross-country runs that formed a large part of the compulsory exercise at

OPPOSITE *Racing at Cowes with Uffa Fox. Although Prince Philip is a keen sailor Prince Charles has never taken whole-heartedly to the sport.*

Timbertop. He rapidly established himself as the leading authority on fishing and was often sought out for advice and instruction by the younger boys. He went on excursions to sheep-stations, where he tried his hand at shearing and left behind what he later admitted to be rather 'shredded sheep'. He went panning for gold and precious stones like the old prospectors. He worked on community-aid schemes similar to those at Gordonstoun, and he spent hours in the gum-forests getting to know the exotic wildlife.

Without doubt his most important goal was winning the friendship and popularity of the other boys, who were different from him in so many ways. Perhaps it was this very difference that presented the challenge, for at Timbertop Charles felt that he would be judged on his own merits as one of the community and not as the future King of Australia. He knew that he had succeeded in this when, one evening, after walking in the rain, he entered the dormitory hut he supervised and was greeted by the delighted cries of 'Pommy bastard' from the fifteen younger boys under his care.

Originally he had come to Timbertop for just one term, but his mother had said that if he enjoyed himself he would be allowed to stay on for one more. Even before his first term had ended, Charles had made up his mind to stay, and his visit to Australia was extended to six months. During the first term he had had the pleasant surprise of seeing his grandmother, while she was on a brief visit to Australia. They spent a few days together, and the Queen Mother was obviously pleased by how much he had grown and how well he was looking. This news and the enthusiastic letters he sent home must have come as a great relief to his parents after the anxieties they had felt earlier in his school career.

Charles displayed similar enthusiasm when he wrote an account of life at Timbertop for the *Gordonstoun Record* under the title 'Timbertop: or Beating About the Bush':

A popular cry seems to be that Timbertop is very similar to Gordonstoun [began the Prince]. From what I make of it, Timbertop is very individual. All the boys are virtually the same age, fourteen to fifteen; there are no prefects, and the masters do all the work that boys might otherwise do in a school. This way I think there is much more contact between masters and boys, as everyone is placed in the same sort of situation.

Apart from its regime of cross-country runs, there were major differences in the daily routine, as Charles quickly discovered:

There is a lot of wood-chopping done here, but I'm afraid it's very essential as the boys' boilers have to be stoked with logs, and the kitchen uses a huge number. The first week I was here I was made to go out and chop up logs on a hillside in boiling hot weather. I could hardly see my hands for blisters after that! Each afternoon after classes, which end at three

OPPOSITE *Prince Charles at Timbertop in 1966, the country extension of Geelong Grammar School in Australia. He liked Timbertop so much he stayed an extra term.*

A smiling Prince Charles enjoys an informal visit to the Scilly Isles which form part of his territory as Duke of Cornwall.

o'clock, there are jobs which are rather equivalent to PW but involve chopping and splitting wood, feeding the pigs, cleaning out fly-traps (which are revolting glass bowls seething with flies and very ancient meat) or picking up bits of paper round the School.

The principal difference between the two schools was the nature of the expeditions at Timbertop, and these obviously fired Charles's enthusiasm.

Some boys manage to walk fantastic distances over a weekend of four days or less, and do 130 or 200 miles [he wrote admiringly]. The furthest I've been is 60–70 miles in three days, climbing about five peaks on the way. At the campsite the cooking is done on an open fire in a trench. You have to be very careful in hot weather that you don't start a bush fire, and at the beginning of this term there was a total fire-ban in force, so that you ate all the tinned food cold.

Charles left Australia with other vivid memories as well, and of these the most important must have been the moment when he felt himself transform from a self-effacing schoolboy into a confident young man. This metamorphosis happened during a refuelling stop-over at Brisbane while he was *en route* for New Guinea. When someone on the plane told him to go out and have an impromptu word with the crowd that had gathered on the tarmac to see him, he was so petrified that he had to be virtually kicked off the plane, but as he walked over to the crowd of beaming faces he suddenly felt something 'click' inside, and from that moment he claims never to have felt awkward in public again.

This unexpected change in his nature clearly influenced his visit to the missionary-stations in New Guinea. No longer afraid of crowds of strangers, Charles was able to concentrate on the new things he witnessed and experienced, forgetting his own self-consciousness. He was profoundly moved by the sincerity in the Christian worship he witnessed among the primitive tribespeople in the territory. He also showed great interest in their ancient traditions and their cultural heritage that he felt was being eroded by the advance of western civilization.

His second term at Timbertop followed the same pattern as the first, though the weather had altered to mid-winter, allowing Charles the opportunity to act as skiing instructor to most of the others. However, A-level studies were now occupying more and more of his time. Throughout his time in Australia he worked consistently at his studies, although he did gain the reputation for spending too long fishing at the expense of the essays he occasionally sent down to masters at the main school at Geelong. He may not have realized it at the time, but the staff at Geelong seemed to be deliberately giving him the chance to work more on his own initiative, rather than as a supervised schoolboy. Left to his own initiative, this proved to be a great success and boosted his self-esteem still further.

When he left Australia, Charles asked David Checketts to read a short message to those who had gathered to say goodbye to him at the airport:

It would be difficult to leave without saying how much I have enjoyed and appreciated my stay in Australia and how touched I have been by the kindness of so many people in making

Prince Charles playing the 'cello with the Elgin Orchestra which was giving a concert for charity. The concert was a sell-out.

these six months such a worthwhile experience. The most wonderful part was the opportunity to travel and see at least some of the country (I hope I shall be able to come back and see the rest) and also the chance to meet so many people, which completes the link with a country I am very sad to be leaving; and yet I shall now be able to visualize Australia in the most vivid terms, after such a marvellous visit.

With these parting words he left the land which he would always regard as his second home, to return to Gordonstoun, where he would continue to mature and develop from schoolboy to student. He can hardly have foreseen that as an adult his popularity in Australia, which increased with each successful tour he made of the country, would make him a natural choice for Governor-General.

Going back to his old school must have been a severe anti-climax after the invigorating change at Timbertop. Still, it was eased by an obvious improvement in his status in the school. In his absence his fellows at Windmill Lodge had voted him 'helper' (Head of House), and during his last two terms at school he was selected as Guardian (Head Boy) of the school, the position his father had held almost thirty years before.

As Guardian his duties were concerned principally with acting as a mediator between the staff and the pupils. He did not have the right to punish other boys, though he was supposed to ensure that everyone fulfilled their reponsibilities to the community in general. On one occasion he interceded on behalf of two boys under the threat of expulsion, arguing that it would be better to keep them at the school to try to assist their reform rather than cast them out to the world in which reform would be far more difficult to achieve. His plea failed, but his stand impressed staff and pupils alike.

Charles sat his A-levels in the summer of 1967 in the worrying knowledge that, of all the thousands of candidates taking the exams up and down the country, he would be the one most in the public eye when the results were published. In the end he had little cause to worry. The examiners awarded him a grade C in French and a grade B in history, with a distinction in the optional history s-level paper. As Charles's years of education and training approached their final phase, the Queen could reflect with justifiable satisfaction that her daring experiment had turned out in the end to be an unqualified success.

4

The Student Prince

A month after his seventeenth birthday, Charles was the subject of discussion at a small dinner-party given by his parents. Though not present himself, he knew that the purpose of the gathering was to decide the future course of his education.

The guests who were invited represented a wide band of national and state opinion. Harold Wilson, the Prime Minister; Michael Ramsay, Archbishop of Canterbury; Sir Charles Wilson, Chairman of the Committee of Vice-Chancellors; Earl Mountbatten, Admiral of the Fleet; Robert Woods, Dean of Windsor; and Sir Michael Adeane, the Queen's private secretary, had all been informed that Charles had expressed a keen interest in going to university. Their task was to decide how best this should be achieved.

The two key questions under discussion were which university Charles should attend and what course of study he should follow. The conversation explored the advantages and disadvantages of the new universities, the 'redbrick' universities and the ancient institutions sometimes unkindly referred to as 'crumbling masonry'. At the same time, the tradition of royal princes' serving in the armed forces had to be borne in mind.

As the hours ticked away past midnight, it became evident that the consensus of opinion was veering towards Charles's attending one of the old universities, and, since he would have already spent five years at school in Scotland, one of the two ancient universities in England became the most likely choice.

Though the former Prince of Wales, later Duke of Windsor, had been to Oxford, Cambridge seemed a more natural choice for Charles. His grandfather had studied there for a time; his cousins the Princes of Gloucester had gone there, and Cambridge was reasonably close to Sandringham, where he could always find a quiet place to retreat for a week-end. In the end it was Charles's favourite great-uncle 'Dickie', Earl Mountbatten, who proposed the ideal formula: 'Trinity College like his grandfather; Dartmouth like his father and grandfather; and then to sea in the Royal Navy, ending up with a command of his own.'

Charles was told over breakfast the next morning and saw no reason to complain. His own inclination tended towards the past and therefore showed a preference for

OPPOSITE *Prince Charles working in the medieval room which he used as a study while at Trinity College, Cambridge.*

An informal picture of the Queen and her eldest son, taken at Windsor.

the older universities. The choice of college and course was decided through the agency of Robert Woods, who was asked by the Queen to sound out the feelings of the heads of a number of Cambridge colleges. The short-list was boiled down to five, with Dr Woods indicating a preference for Trinity, his old college and the one to which he had sent his sons, whom Charles already knew. Apart from agreeing with Uncle Dickie's proposition, the Royal Family was pleased by the choice in other respects. The Master, Lord Butler, was a well-known and trusted friend of the Queen's, and the college itself drew a large number of its students from state schools, even admitting a few women. At Trinity, Charles would have the chance to mix with a wider variety of people his own age, while belonging to an ancient college with close family ties. A year after the dinner-party at Buckingham Palace it was announced that the Prince of Wales had been offered a place at Trinity for the following year. All that remained now was to finalize the course of study the Prince would follow.

At first Charles had favoured a multi-disciplinary course, and his father, who had never experienced the restrictions of an Honours degree syllabus, probably agreed with him. Prince Philip doubtless cherished the hope that Cambridge might inspire his son with some of the interest he himself felt in technology and studies orientated towards the future. However, this was not to be. After speaking with the Master and the Senior Tutor, Charles decided to spend his first year reading for the Part One Tripos in archaeology and social anthropology. These were subjects in which he had long been interested, and they left open the door to his real passion, history.

There were other considerations to be taken into account over and above the nature of his academic work. Since his education had so far been modelled on that of any boy from a normal upper-middle-class background, it was only right that as a student this should continue to be the case as well. Here again, though, he would be breaking with royal tradition.

Admittedly both Edward VII and Edward VIII had attended university as Princes of Wales, and Charles's grandfather had studied briefly at university when he was Prince Albert, but their circumstances were very different from those of their contemporaries. Apart from lacking any formal qualification to enter the universities (Charles did at least meet the matriculation requirements), they were set apart from the rest of the student body in other ways.

The future Edward VII had lived in his own house in Oxford to which university professors came to teach the royal 'commoner' and half a dozen carefully selected aristocrats. When he was out in the town, he had to wear the gold-tuffed cap and special gown that distinguished him as a nobleman, and when he entered a room frequented by other students, be it common-room or lecture-hall, they were expected to rise to their feet. He later spent a somewhat happier spell at Cambridge, though he never took a degree at either university.

The future Edward VIII, on the other hand, insisted on at least living in his college, Magdalen, but that was about as far as normality went. He soon established a reputation for being a 'gay blade' and seemed to spend most of his time beagling, gambling and attending inebriate dinner-parties. Again neither he nor his brother Bertie (George VI) took degrees.

So, as far as Charles was concerned, he had not only to set a precedent for royal undergraduates, he had also to live down many of the excesses and shortcomings of his predecessors. This may have guided him in his decision to have at least the option to take a degree, and it almost certainly instilled in him the necessity of living in the college like most of the other students. His 'pioneering' will certainly make life easier for Prince Edward who has been the most academically successful of all the Queen's children and has been considering following Charles to Cambridge.

The day he went for his interview, he and his father also inspected his future rooms in a quiet part of New Court, next to the River Cam. His mother later went to see the rooms herself and made certain that she spent some time talking with Charles's 'bedder', or cleaner. The only concessions made to the Prince were a telephone and a small kitchen which was converted for him by workmen from Sandringham.

As at every other stage of his education, there were voices raised in protest at the news that Charles was going to Cambridge. Many critics were convinced that rank alone had won him one of the most coveted university places in the country. When his A-level results were announced, a motion was tabled at the annual conference of the National Union of Students, which sarcastically congratulated him on his 'success' and on his 'rare good fortune' in being awarded a place at Cambridge on two A-levels. They also asked to know how many other students had been accepted by universities on the merit of results like his and in particular how many had been accepted by Cambridge colleges. The Prince's only possible answer was to show that he merited his place on his performance at university. This meant that for the entire three years he spent at Cambridge he was under greater pressure to do well than almost any other undergraduate.

He arrived at the gates of Trinity in October 1967. In spite of his low-key arrival in David Checketts's mini, there was the inevitable crowd waiting to see him greeted

On his first day at Cambridge, Charles was shown around the college grounds and library by Robert Woods, another undergraduate.

by Lord Butler and Dennis Marrian, who had been appointed his tutor.

As he was escorted into the college, the porters manned the magnificent wooden gates to keep out the crowd. 'Good luck,' a voice shouted after him. 'Thanks,' the Prince shouted back, 'I'll need it,' and with that the gates thudded shut behind him.

In spite of the strange surroundings, for about the first time in his life Charles was in a place where he wholeheartedly wanted to be. Before him stretched the prospect of studying subjects that had interested him for years. He had freedom to explore traditional haunts about which he had read and heard so much, and perhaps for the first and last time in his life he was presented with the opportunity to mix casually with people his own age on a more or less equal footing.

These were worthy ideals, but they proved to be hard to achieve in reality, for, although his surroundings and circumstances were clearly more comfortable and relaxed than at either Cheam or Gordonstoun, the old problem of his identity still remained.

Like other freshmen he donned his gown and went to the Great Hall to dine; like other freshmen he was debited six shillings (30p) before he sat down to eat, and like the others he munched his way through the bland institutional meals. However, he was still clearly a source of either blatant curiosity or studied indifference. The by now familiar reticence among his fellows at Trinity that prevented many of them from befriending him, was matched by the deliberate indifference of others. It was a time of widespread student discontent with the establishment, at home and abroad, and the company of princes did nothing to enhance the status of aspiring left-wing radicals. The strain of these meals soon drove Charles to eating in his own room. Lord Butler's wise advice about the kitchen had provided the means for cooking for himself, while a service existed for students to have meals sent up from the college kitchens, provided they were prepared to pay.

It became clear after a time too that he preferred to choose his friends from among the sons of the landed gentry and from the polo-playing fraternity, like himself products of public schools. This must have been a disappointment to those who had hoped that he might get to know some of the hundreds of state-educated undergraduates who were at Trinity at the same time. However, no one could dictate whom the Prince should choose as friends, and he naturally veered towards those with whom he had the most in common.

He quickly won a half-blue in polo, representing the university against the team from Oxford, and he formed an all-male dining-club called 'the Wapiti Society' with others of similar interests and backgrounds. As a member of this coterie he occasionally indulged in harmless student pranks, such as riding bicycles round the courtyard after midnight, and he was not averse to disregarding certain university rules, such as the one that prevented students' keeping cars at Cambridge during their first year and driving in the city at any time. Lord Butler was often amused to

OVERLEAF *Charles shopping in a Cambridge street market.*

While at Cambridge Charles made his first solo flight. He is pictured here with one of his flying instructors, squadron leader Peter Pinney.

watch him walking purposively out of the college to the waiting Land-Rover driven by his detective in the certain knowledge that they were on the way to collect the Prince's MGB sportscar, discreetly hidden somewhere in the vicinity.

But, if Lord Butler turned a blind eye to these minor infringements of student discipline, he was certainly mindful of the responsibilities and duties that Charles would have in later life. The Prince must have counted himself very fortunate to have the Master as his mentor during his three years at Trinity. Lord Butler cleared three-quarters of an hour each evening for the Prince to visit him, and during their evening discussions he gave Charles the benefit of his experience gained in posts as varied as Deputy Prime Minister, Home Secretary and Chancellor of the Exchequer. The rapport that grew between the insatiably curious student and the one-time Cabinet Minister was a major achievement of Charles's time at Cambridge. As Lord Butler watched the future monarch mature in his opinions and attitudes, he was able to guide and instruct him in the difficult processes of royal conduct and standing.

When Charles called on him one evening to ask whether it would be all right for him to join the University Labour Club, Butler had to explain tactfully that the monarchy had to remain politically neutral. Realizing the severe limitations that

Prince Charles fishing in Dorset. The Prince has learned a great deal from his fellow fishing enthusiast, the Queen Mother.

this placed on an intelligent, thinking young man, surrounded by a hubbub of political activity, he did encourage him to continue his political discussions in private. Consequently Charles spent many evenings arguing late into the night with a Welsh student, Hywel Jones, who lived on the same staircase. Though of very different political and social complexions, the two young men established a firm friendship and mutual respect. Their meetings may also have inspired the Prince to put on a disguise for the only time in his life, when he went to attend his first – and last – student demonstration to see what they were like.

Towards the end of his second term he was asked to contribute to the university newspaper, *Varsity*, which was celebrating its twenty-first birthday. Writing about his first impressions of life in Cambridge, he happened to comment on the singing of one of the dustmen outside his window early in the morning: this, he confided, was one of the less mellifluous sounds of Cambridge. Such was the effect of the royal notice that the singing dustman was immediately tracked down and offered a recording contract, while in deference to the Prince of Wales's slumbers the refuse-collection was delayed until nine o'clock.

If Charles was little in evidence around Cambridge during his first year, it was as a

Despite the many demands on his time while at Cambridge, Prince Charles found time to indulge his interest in amateur dramatics and he was a popular performer in college revues.

result of diligence not default. He worked hard at his chosen subjects and impressed his tutors by his keenness and interest in what he was learning. In the vacation before his first exams he travelled with an archaeological party to France and Jersey, showing the same enthusiasm for dank caves and primitive dwellings as he had first displayed in the wind-swept shelters of prehistoric Morayshire. The result of this application to his work was justly rewarded with an Upper Second in his first-year Tripos exams, a result which was considerably better than average.

As with many students, Charles's second year was partly a time of experiment and enjoyment before the cloud of finals loomed on the horizon. Taking to the stage once again, he delighted audiences by his first performance in Joe Orton's play *Erpingham Camp*, when, as a vicar in a holiday camp, he ended up with a very liberally filled custard pie being flung right into his face. However, his real comic talent emerged in the college revues, which appealed to his slightly way-out sense of humour. As a long-standing fan of the Goons, Charles exploited every opportunity to employ their brand of zany comedy. He was perfectly happy also to laugh at himself, and many of the funniest sketches were self-mocking ones.

In his first revue *Revolution* he appeared in fourteen of the forty sketches. Entering beneath an opened umbrella, he announced, 'I lead a sheltered life.' Later in the evening he left the stage with a young lady on his arm and a wicked look in his eye saying: 'I like to give myself airs.' He impersonated the Master of Trinity, the Duke of Wellington and a certain singing dustman, who appeared sitting in a

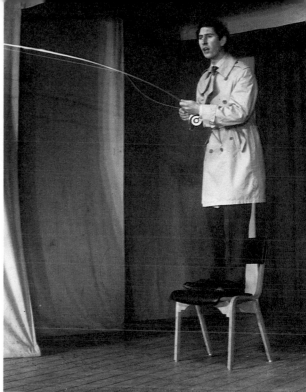

dustbin being interviewed by the media and charging £5 for the privilege. His performances were so popular that in the next production there was scarcely one sketch that did not feature the Prince on stage.

He did not let this interfere with his studies however. Having passed his Part Ones with such success, he was advised by many people to continue with archaeology and anthropology, since he might conceivably have achieved a First in his finals. However, Charles had made up his mind to change to the history course for the second part of the Tripos, a not unfitting topic for a future King of Great Britain. In this he displayed characteristic diligence. At the same time, apart from his other interests, polo, the 'cello and acting, he was being called upon more and more to fulfil what Lord Butler scathingly referred to as 'balcony jobs'. Whether he liked it or not, Charles had only a few more months before he was due to be launched as a fully fledged public figure in his own right.

The middle 1960s had been a troubled time for Wales. While other areas of Great Britain seemed at last to be experiencing a rise in living-standards, the Principality still appeared to be a forgotten economic backwater, with its traditional industries facing closure or growing competition from overseas. This mood of discontent was given added momentum by the horrific disaster of a coal-tip's slide onto a school at Aberfan on 21 October 1966, killing many children. When seven months after the tragedy it was announced that the Queen would invest the Prince of Wales at Caernarvon Castle in the summer of 1969, the news acted as a catalyst for all the Welsh discontent.

Welsh nationalism became the cry in the mountains and valleys. Small radical

Official duties took up an increasing amount of the Prince's time while he was a student. He is shown here before leaving to attend a funeral service in Australia with Harold Wilson and during his first State Opening of Parliament, in 1967 (right).

bands began attacking government installations with bombs, and others started issuing threats against the lives of the Royal Family in general and Prince Charles in particular. It was becoming clear that the Investiture would have to be handled with great tact and diplomacy. The announcement, in November 1967, that Prince Charles would be spending the summer term prior to the Investiture studying Welsh at the University College of Wales, at Aberystwyth, only brought more arguments into the conflict.

There were many who felt that this was a totally unjustifiable interruption of his degree course. There were others who saw it as a move by the government to try to win favour with the disaffected Welsh electorate. Then of course there was the chorus of Welsh protest that saw the Prince as a cheap pawn in the game of English imperialism. And right in the middle there was a twenty-year-old history student about to be plucked from his cloistered seclusion, to be flung, if not to the lions, at least to the red dragon. In all this furore Charles himself adopted a commendably calm attitude towards what looked like being the sternest test he had yet faced. Interviewed on the radio, he had this to say on the subject:

I expect at Aberystwyth there may be one or two demonstrations, and as long as I don't get covered too much in egg and tomato I'll be all right, but I don't blame people demonstrating

like that. They've never seen me before, they don't know what I'm like. I've hardly been to Wales, and you can't really expect people to be over-zealous about the fact of having a so-called English Prince to come amongst them and be frightfully excited. Once I've been there for eight weeks things might improve.

For all his dignified *sang froid* though, the Prince must have had worries for his safety. His parents certainly had, and as the start of the term approached, the tension mounted around their son. There were student demonstrations organized against his visit, and an anti-royalist pop-song reached the top of the Welsh hit-parade with these inspired lyrics:

> I have a friend who lives in Buckingham Palace
> And Carlo Windsor is his name.
> The last time I went round to his house
> His mother answered the door and said:
> 'Carlo, Carlo, Carlo is playing polo today
> Carlo is playing with his Dad.'
> So come all ye serfs of Wales and join in the chorus.
> At last you have a Prince in the land of song.

'Carlo' is a popular Welsh name for a dog, and many of the cartoons of the Prince at that time depicted him as a faithful lap-dog of the government.

Four days before Charles's arrival at Aberystwyth, nine members of the Free Wales Army had gone on trial accused of bombings that had taken place during the last eighteen months. Their trial ended on 1 July, the day of the Investiture.

By the time Charles arrived at the start of the summer term, Aberystwyth had been placed under a huge security-net. Some Special Branch men had enrolled as students to keep an eye on the Prince, while others lived in the town keeping an ear to the ground. But Charles's own conduct during that trying period did much to ease the tension. On the first day he amazed security officers and townspeople alike by going shopping and chatting casually with people in the streets. He was careful frequently to let drop the few Welsh words that he had learned before arriving. He was equally careful afterwards to keep well out of the limelight while he acquired a more substantial grasp of the language in the university's language laboratories.

From his tutor, ardent Welsh nationalist Edward Millward, he learned much of Welsh history and literature, of which he admitted he knew next to nothing. He learned of the last Welsh Prince of Wales, Llewelyn ap Gruffydd, of whom he had displayed woeful ignorance when he once asked an angry Welsh protestor who the Llewelyn was on his placard.

Eight weeks after starting work on the language, Charles addressed the Welsh League of Youth at its Eisteddfod in Aberystwyth. He spoke fluently in the difficult language for several minutes without making a single mistake. The effect was magical. The audience applauded him warmly and christened him '*cariad bach*' – 'little darling'. Moderate Welsh opinion began to hold sway, and the tide of anti-

20 April 1969. Charles arrives at Aberystwyth for a nerve-racking term at the University of Wales in preparation for his Investiture.

Investiture feeling began to turn.

The first ordeal was over. The Welsh had had an opportunity to see a little more of their Prince, and they had not found him wanting – though in their hide-outs in the northern mountains the descendants of Llewelyn's last army were preparing their final show of defiance. Charles had now reached the ultimate test in his twenty years of careful preparation. The self-confidence and self-control that he had struggled to acquire through the sometimes painful years at Cheam and Gordonstoun were now to be put to the test.

At the Investiture he would be exposed before a crowd of ten thousand and a television audience of five hundred million. Even more frightening though was the very real possibility that he might also be standing in the direct line of an assassin's gun-sight.

Edward 'the Black Prince', the third English Prince of Wales, was the first to carry all the titles and adopt the motto which Charles was due to inherit. But there were other similarities that joined the two young men across the span of history: even in the twentieth century the Prince of Wales would be called upon to display all his personal resources of will-power and courage, before being accepted as a worthy successor to Llewelyn's title.

Edward had won his spurs at Crécy. Charles would win his in a less spectacular manner at Caernarvon.

5

The Investiture

The connection between the English Princes of Wales and the town of Caernarvon dates back to the thirteenth century. According to the traditional account, King Edward I of England presented his infant son to the Welsh barons at Caernarvon and proclaimed him Prince of Wales. The line of the ancient Welsh princes was thereby ended and the English line begun. From that moment the Welsh were to regard Caernarvon as a symbol of the English occupation of their country and national sovereignty.

Ironically, it was a Welshman, David Lloyd George, who was instrumental in 're-enacting' this piece of historical make-believe in 1911. Realizing that such a royal pageant would greatly enhance his own political prestige as well as act as a fitting conclusion to King George V's Coronation tour of the realm, the then Chancellor of the Exchequer persuaded the King once again to present a newly invested Prince of Wales to his subjects at Caernarvon.

For Lloyd George the Investiture of Prince Edward, later King Edward VIII, was a masterpiece of political opportunism. For the Prince it was little short of a nightmare. As a seventeen-year-old naval cadet at Dartmouth, he was forced to endure far greater ridicule from his friends as a result of the ceremony than that already suggested by his nickname 'Sardine'. Apart from the fact that the Prince intensely disliked pomp and pageantry anyway, it had been decided that he should speak to his subjects in their own notoriously difficult language. To make matters worse, he was forced to wear a costume that in his opinion must have been more fitting for a pantomime or a production of Gilbert and Sullivan's *Iolanthe* than a serious public ceremony.

Many years later, writing as Duke of Windsor, he recalled his feelings on that boiling hot July day in 1911, when, wearing 'a fantastic costume designed for the occasion, consisting of white satin breeches and a mantle and surcoat of purple velvet edged with ermine', he was paraded at Caernarvon:

...with Winston Churchill as Home Secretary mellifluously proclaiming my titles (he told me afterwards that he rehearsed them on a golf-course), my father invested me as Prince of Wales. Upon my head he put a coronet cap as token of principality, and into my hand the

OPPOSITE *Prince Charles in his Investiture robes which were worn over a conventional military uniform.*

gold verge of government, and on the middle finger the gold ring of responsibility. Then, leading me by the hand through the archway to one of the towers of the battlements, he presented me to the people of Wales. Half fainting with heat and nervousness, I delivered the Welsh sentence that Mr Lloyd George, standing close by in the ancient garb of Constable, had taught me.

No doubt aware of these views of his great-uncle, Charles can be forgiven if he felt some misgivings about the nature of the ceremony in the period leading up to his own Investiture.

If he had doubts about it though, he was not alone. Protests were raised in Wales against the Investiture for two main reasons: firstly because many Welsh people saw it as merely a means of 'rubber-stamping' the so-called English occupation of their country by a piece of royal pageantry, and secondly because in their opinion it was a scandalous waste of government money. Wales needed industrial investment and social improvement, the nationalists claimed. The last thing they wanted was a 'royal circus'.

There were others, on the opposite side of the fence, who to some extent shared this point of view. One of the most influential of them was none other than the Queen. Her Majesty had long felt that the Investiture of her uncle in 1911 had been far too elaborate, and she was adamant that such ceremony would be completely out of place over half a century later. She was all for trimming the costs wherever possible and went as far as vetoing the original proposal that the budget should be £500,000. The estimate was lowered to £200,000, but even this did not prevent some

Edward, Prince of Wales (later Edward VIII), in his Investiture costume just prior to the ceremony in 1911. The whole ceremony and in particular the anachronistic costume with its white satin knee breeches was a terrible embarrassment to the Prince.

critics asserting that the whole exercise was designed to increase the prestige of the Royal Family, with an idea of gaining an increase in the amount of money granted in the Civil List.

The preparations began in earnest twenty months before the actual event. A huge committee was gathered under the chairmanship of the Duke of Norfolk, who as Earl Marshall had master-minded the Queen's Coronation sixteen years before. A traditionalist by nature, he warned his committee that 'there would be no monkeying about in the name of modernization.' The ceremony itself would be a carbon copy of that laid down constitutionally for the Investiture in 1911. However, the modern gloss of the 1960s was tastefully introduced by the designs of Lord Snowdon, who, as Constable of Caernarvon Castle, was selected to supervise the staging of the ceremony.

Snowdon's two guiding principles were that the setting should be simple and that the proceedings should be easily visible from all sides. The latter was particularly important, since for the first time in its history the Investiture of the Prince of Wales was to be viewed by a world-wide television audience.

Many aesthetic improvements had already been made to the castle before the work for the Investiture itself was started, which meant that Lord Snowdon was able to continue work he had already begun. He designed the ceremony around a plain circular dais of grey slate, which, like all the materials and furnishings, came from within the Principality. Above this was a canopy of perspex supported on steel poles shaped like lances, which gave the appearance of a medieval tent. Capable of withstanding sixty-mile-an-hour winds, this bold concession to modern technology also gave an excellent view to both the television cameras and the four thousand spectators seated around the fifty tons of specially laid turf on which the ceremony would take place.

In spite of the efforts to economize, a public opinion poll held in Wales ten months before the Investiture revealed that forty-four per cent of the people thought that it was a waste of public money. The Welsh Nationalist Party, Plaid Cymru, with one Westminster MP and forty-thousand members, decided to boycott the entire proceedings, while the Welsh Language Society began their own idiosyncratic campaign. English place-names were painted over on many Welsh signposts, and anti-Investiture graffiti appeared in Welsh on bridges and hoardings. However, the hard-line Free Wales Army began a far more dangerous campaign of gelignite and terror: their first bomb was exploded in the Cardiff Temple of Peace at the time when over four hundred Welshmen were gathering to discuss plans for the Investiture in November 1967. No one was hurt, but the damage amounted to £30,000. During the next twenty months leading up to the ceremony they exploded twelve other bombs damaging various government buildings, a police station, RAF installations and a pipeline carrying water to large English cities.

However, the weeks immediately preceding the Investiture saw a distinct swing in public opinion in its favour. This was due to a sudden rise in the popularity of the

Prince Edward is taken for a go-cart ride by a protective elder brother in the grounds of Windsor Castle.

monarchy brought about in part by the television film *Royal Family*. Charles had himself received very favourable reviews from the film and, following the great personal success of his eight weeks at Aberystwyth, had won all but the most militant Welsh hearts. Even some of his most trenchant opponents had been impressed by his good humour and integrity in the face of insults and threats. The Mayor of Caernarvon, who had originally been one of the greatest sceptics, no doubt expressed the opinions of many Welsh people when he spoke of the Prince in glowing terms, calling him 'the ace in the royal pack'.

Despite this dramatic swing in popular opinion, the bombings and threats continued right up to 1 July, and in the end the security precautions which had to be stringently enforced accounted for over one tenth of the total budget.

Travelling to Wales overnight in the purple-painted royal train, the Royal Family were delayed for one hour at Crewe, while a bomb further up the line was defused. In the end it turned out to be a hoax, but in the tension of the moment the two sticks of plasticine and the alarm-clock were viewed as far from a practical joke. During the night, while the Royal Family slept in a secluded siding, the security services maintained a constant check on the railway line leading to the point where the Queen and other members would leave the train. Though no bomb was found, their vigilance was certainly needed, since around dawn a real bomb was being planted

May 1969. David Frost interviews Prince Charles at home in a television programme entitled 'A Prince for Wales', made during the run-up to the Investiture.

outside the government offices in Abergele, inland from Colwyn Bay. As the two terrorists were priming it, the home made device exploded, killing them both. The Free Wales Army could now claim two martyrs for its cause.

Throughout the day the carefully co-ordinated security operation monitored the whole proceedings. Police in rubber dinghies patrolled the Menai Straits, looking for possible bombs. The gathering crowds were infiltrated by security men all along the procession route and at the base of the castle walls. Helicopters hovered five hundred feet above their heads, observing any suspicious action, and television cameras kept the milling throng under constant surveillance. Even the royal yacht *Britannia* was considered a potential target, and frogmen frequently inspected her hull throughout the day, looking for limpet-mines.

The Queen and her family were entertained to a champagne breakfast by Sir Michael Duff, the Lord Lieutenant of Caernarvon, at his mansion overlooking the Menai Straits. But in spite of the genial atmosphere, the tension within the family group was obvious. Prince Charles spent the morning pacing around the grounds of the estate, and the occasional sight of security guards could have done nothing to reassure him. Returning to the house on one occasion, he caught sight of an interview he had given on television that was being shown as a preview to the afternoon's ceremony. 'It's always me,' he commented.

After lunch he set out with the first part of the procession, accompanied by David Checketts and the Secretary of State for Wales, George Thomas. As their coach rattled through the crowded streets of Caernarvon, escorted by the Household Cavalry, the area near the processional route suddenly echoed with a loud explosion. Another bomb had gone off – fortunately, this time, injuring no one.

However, the air was soon filled with other, more welcome sounds. As the Prince approached the castle, the trumpets from the Household Cavalry sounded a fanfare from the battlements as the Prince of Wales's banner was unfurled over the Eagle Tower. The fanfare then faded away, only to be replaced by the crowd's spontaneously breaking into 'God Bless the Prince of Wales' as Charles walked to the Chamberlain Tower, where he would wait to be summoned for his Investiture.

The only incident that occurred during the procession of the rest of the Royal Family threatened the safety of the protestor himself rather more than his intended victim. A young man who had thrown a banana-skin under the hoofs of the horses drawing the royal coach, in the hope that they might slip, had so infuriated those standing next to him that the police took him away as much for his own safety as for the need to charge him with insulting behaviour.

When the Queen arrived at the castle, she was greeted by the Constable of the Castle, Lord Snowdon, holding an enormous key. After formally entrusting the key once again to her brother-in-law's care, the Queen and the royal party made their way to the dais and the three simple thrones of grey Welsh slate. The Welsh and English National Anthems were played, and the Garter King of Arms was sent to fetch the Prince in order to begin the ceremony.

Dressed in the uniform of the Colonel-in-Chief of the newly created Royal Regiment of Wales, Charles appeared bare-headed, flanked by the Secretary of State for Wales, the Wales Herald Extraordinary and two attendant peers. Behind him walked five Welsh peers bearing the insignia of Investiture: the silver-gilt sword, the golden rod signifying authority, the ring, with which the Prince would be married to his country, the mantle of purple silk velvet and ermine, and the coronet. As the Queen invested her son with these insignia, the Letters Patent which created Charles Prince of Wales were read first in English by the Home Secretary, James Callaghan and then in Welsh by George Thomas.

Then came the moving climax to the ceremony. Kneeling at his mother's feet, Charles placed his hands between the Queen's and declared: 'I, Charles, Prince of Wales, do become your liege man of life and limb and of earthly worship, and faith and truth I will bear unto you to live and die against all manner of folks.' The Queen raised him to his feet, and they exchanged the kiss of fealty.

Then Sir Bowen Thomas, President of Aberystwyth university, gave the loyal address in Welsh, while the newly invested Prince fumbled anxiously beneath his robes to locate his own speech on which he had accidentally sat. He then replied in both Welsh and English, promising 'to associate myself in word and deed with as much of the life of the Principality as possible'.

There then followed a short service conducted in both languages, after which the Queen led her son to the castle battlements where she presented him to the people of Wales. Trumpeters sounded their fanfare across the roofs of the town; the RAF flew in formation high overhead, and the cheering crowds might have been saluting a victorious rugby team in Cardiff Arms Park for all the noise of the cheering.

What had been seen by many as a royal blunder of the first degree had turned out to be a splendid triumph. The Welsh were enthralled with their new Prince. During the four-day tour of his Principality which followed, he received the same ecstatic reception from thousands of ardent supporters, who saw in him a man whom they knew would more than live up to the motto 'Ich dien' ('I serve') which he had inherited from the Black Prince. He was now a full member of what his grandfather had been in the habit of referring to as 'the royal firm'.

It was only a short time after the Investiture that Charles first demonstrated his concern for the welfare of his people. On the final day of his tour of Wales, while he was in Cardiff, an eleven-year-old schoolboy, innocently kicking around a football, detonated a booby-trap bomb and lost one of his legs. The tragedy cast a cloud over Charles's buoyant spirits. He was very keen to visit the boy in hospital, but the doctors felt that the royal visit might over-excite him after his major operation and advised the Prince to write to him instead, which Charles did. When an appeal fund was set up, he made a sizeable contribution.

1 July 1969. The Prince arrives at Caernarvon Castle for his Investiture as Prince of Wales.

OPPOSITE ABOVE The Prince kneels in front of his mother the Queen during the Investiture ceremony in order to pay homage to her.

OPPOSITE BELOW The Standard of the Prince of Wales which is flown only when the Prince is in Wales.

ABOVE Watched by the Queen the Prince steadies the coronet which she has just placed on his head as a symbol of his authority as Prince of Wales.

LEFT A young Welsh protestor is led away by police after an incident in the crowd as the Queen's procession moved towards Caernarvon Castle.

Before entering into full public service, Charles had still one private task to complete for himself and for his parents. He had still to sit for his university degree.

It must have been a tremendous relief to get back to Trinity that October, after the emotional strain of the term at Aberystwyth and the Investiture. With a much fuller programme of official engagements in the year ahead and his final examinations in the early summer, Charles got his head down right away. He knew that there was no time to lose, and he knew that he could not afford a bad degree.

He did allow himself a little respite for his twenty-first birthday though. Some of his fellow-students climbed onto the roofs opposite his windows and draped a banner three-hundred-feet long between two of the college's tallest towers, bearing the greeting 'Happy Birthday, Charles'. What they did not know was that the Prince had returned to London the previous evening to spend his birthday with his family.

Four hundred guests were invited to a birthday party at the Palace, and were entertained by Yehudi Menuhin and the Bath Festival Orchestra playing a Mozart violin concerto. This was followed by a concerto on the Prince's favourite instrument, the 'cello. After fireworks in the Palace gardens, the party danced to a pop-group, the Three Degrees, until breakfast, which was served at three o'clock in the morning.

Back at Cambridge the hours of work continued as the period of revision loomed nearer. Charles allowed himself occasional visits to the Cambridge Union to attend the debates, and he did manage to appear in his last review *Quiet Flows the Don*, but like most third-year undergraduates his time was spent mainly in working for his degree.

As he had anticipated, this last year was not to be free of official interruptions, which must have been great distractions to the conscientious history-finalist. On 11 February 1970 he was introduced into the House of Lords by his two sponsors, the Duke of Kent and the Duke of Beaufort. As Charles entered Parliament he doffed his cap three times as he bowed three times to the empty throne and then proceeded to swear allegiance to his mother and paradoxically to himself: 'I, Charles, Prince of Wales, do swear by Almighty God that I will be faithful and bear true allegiance to Her Majesty Queen Elizabeth, her heirs and successors, so help me God.' Once the formalities were over, the Prince removed his peers' robes of scarlet and ermine and returned in a plain suit to listen to the debate, which appropriately was on youth and community service.

In April he was sworn in as a member of the Privy Council, another step towards his involvement in affairs of state. During the Easter vacation he was called upon to join the royal tour of Australia and New Zealand, to celebrate the bicentenary of the voyage of Captain Cook to the Antipodes. Though at other times the opportunity to enjoy the surfing and other pleasures of his 'second home' would have been very attractive, the nagging anxiety of what awaited him in Cambridge must have made the tour more of a frustration than a pleasure.

Before returning home, Charles flew to Japan for five days to undertake his first

Prince Charles chats to a worker on the Vauxhall section of London's new Jubilee underground railway line.

mission abroad on his own. He visited the Expo 70 and dined with Emperor Hirohito, thus easing the path for the visit by his parents to the country five years later. In Kyoto he toured the famous temples of the old capital city, sat cross-legged eating a meal on the straw mat and enjoyed the soothing massage offered by an obliging geisha girl. It was during this visit to Japan that he also scored the first of his trade successes. While talking with the head of the massive Sony electronics company, Charles discovered that they were considering building a factory in western Europe. The Prince of Wales urged the Sony president to consider constructing the plant in his Principality, and four years later he must have felt a great sense of satisfaction when he was invited to open the new Sony factory in Glamorgan, bringing new sources of employment to a badly depressed area. He had shown he was a Prince of Wales in action as well as in words.

Only four weeks after being fêted by the heads of the industrial world in Japan, Charles was one of hundreds of candidates trooping into the Old Schools in Cambridge to sit six three-hour papers of the Part Two Tripos in history. When the results were published later in the summer, his tutor, Dr Marrian, telephoned the Palace with the news that the Prince had been awarded a Lower Second class degree. It was an unexceptional result, but it had been achieved in far from normal circumstances, and both Prince and tutor were delighted with his degree. There were some cynics who suggested that the examiners had shown favouritism in marking the Prince's papers, but this idea was quickly dismissed as impossible by Lord Butler, who pointed out that the history examiners had no idea whose papers they were marking. He went on to say that in his opinion Charles might have got an Upper Second if his final year had not been so interrupted by his royal duties and reiterated what he had said two years before, that if Charles had stuck to archaeology and anthropology he might even have got a First. Now that his education had finished, however, the public was waiting expectantly for the Prince to make his mark on the nation and the world at large.

The time had come for him to put into practice the edicts of his simple motto. It was time to serve.

OPPOSITE *Prince Charles wearing the traditional undergraduate's gown.*

6

The Serving Prince

Although Charles's years at school had been an unprecedented departure from previous royal practice, there had been nothing unusual in Earl Mountbatten's suggestion that he should spend some time in the Royal Navy. In joining the Senior Service, he would be following a long-standing family tradition. There had been one notable alteration made to Lord Louis's scheme, and that was the decision to train Charles as an RAF pilot before he went to sea. Apart from being an acknowledgement of the key rôle that the Air Force plays in the modern defence of Britain, this decision also reflected Charles's own enthusiasm for flying, which was to feature throughout his period in the armed forces.

Needless to say, there were many critics who complained, as they were later to do again when Prince Andrew chose the same course, that the Service traditions of the Royal Family were anachronistic and war-mongering. But Charles was a strong advocate of the tradition and defended it in one speech, saying:

It is pointless and ill-informed to say that I am entering a profession of killing. The Services in the first place are there for fast, efficient and well trained action in defence. Surely the Services must attract a large number of duty-conscious people? Otherwise who else would subject themselves to being square-bashed, shouted at by petty officers and made to do ghastly things in force-ten gales? I am entering the RAF and then the Navy because I believe I can contribute something to this country by so doing. To me it is a worthwhile occupation and one I am convinced will stand me in good stead for the rest of my life.

Charles had started flying, with his father's encouragement, during his first long vacation at Cambridge. He continued his lessons in a Chipmunk of the Queen's Flight, in which he made his first solo flight in January 1969. Describing his feelings later he expressed the feelings shared by all pilots when they leave the ground for the first time:

I always thought I was going to be terrified. I was dreading the moment throughout training when I would have to go up alone. But on the day I went solo, the instructor taxied up to the end of the runway and suddenly climbed out and said: 'You're on your own, mate!' So there I was, and I hardly had time to get butterflies in my tummy before taking off. I was wondering whether I could do it, but the moment I was in the air it was absolutely

OPPOSITE *One of the many portrait photographs taken of the Prince in uniform during his military career.*

marvellous. There was no instructor to breath down my neck, and the aeroplane flew much better because he had gone and the weight was not there. I had a wonderful time. Fortunately, I landed well the first time. That had been the only thing worrying me during the flight. I had visions of my going around and around until eventually the fuel ran out. But all was well.

A little over a year later he was awarded a Grade A private pilot's licence.

Thanks to this previous flying experience and his degree from Cambridge, Charles was able to enter the RAF's shortened graduate-training programme and undertake it in a mere five months. In a stylish act of bravado he flew himself to the RAF College at Cranwell at the controls of a twin-engined Beagle Basset, already wearing the uniform of a flight-lieutenant.

After entering the Service on an equal footing with other ex-student cadets, Charles was more than a little disappointed to learn that he was to be given special treatment. Code-named 'Golden Eagle' and described as a 'precious piece of the nation's property', he was assigned two Mark V Jet Provosts specially adapted with extra warning lights on the control panel and an improved ejector seat. Even so, Charles soon discovered that learning to fly jet aircraft in five months is no easy task, and by the end of his training he had grown to understand the significance of the RAF motto 'Per Ardua Ad Astra' – 'Through effort to the Stars'.

The months at Cranwell were packed with intensive courses, all of which Charles had to pass in sequence before being allowed to move on to the next stage. He learned dinghy drill in the swimming-bath, parachute landing in the gym and technical details about aircraft in the classrooms and workshops. His limited mathematical powers were stretched to their limits by the constant calculations he had to make. He was expected to be able to perform complicated arithmetic in his head, and the solutions to algebraic problems and geometrical formulae were supposed to be at his fingertips. But even these old adversaries were eventually overcome by Charles's diligence and a good deal of painstaking toil, and he managed to pass the courses in aeronautics and navigation in which maths plays such an important part.

It was not only his mind that was taxed by the flying. As a prospective jet pilot, he had to accustom his body to the great demands that would be put on it by flying at supersonic speeds and at high altitudes. One test was designed to simulate the loss of oxygen supply at twenty-thousand feet. Locked inside a decompression chamber, he was made to write simple sentences for several minutes, while on the verge of blacking-out. This excruciating exercise was designed to teach the pilot to recognize the symptoms of such a failure in the air. Apparently Charles's scribblings accurately reflected the intense discomfort he underwent, and these have been carefully filed away until an official biographer finally reveals the Prince of Wales's command of some of the more colourful phrases of the Queen's English!

Although, as Charles openly admitted, his technical acumen was inferior to that of the other cadets, he quickly displayed his natural talent for flying when he was

Having learnt to fly while at Cambridge, Prince Charles trained at Cranwell to qualify as a pilot of jet planes.

seated at the controls of an aircraft. After only three weeks on the course he made his first flight in a jet Provost, and his first solo flight in the 480-mph aircraft followed only a couple of weeks later. In fact, he made this solo after only eight hours' instruction, as opposed to the customary ten.

From Provosts he moved on to flying many of the frontline aircraft used in Britain's air-defences. He took part in an interception exercise over the North Sea, co-piloting a Phantom, and during the same flight helped to perform the difficult manoeuvre of refuelling in mid-air. On the return to the Phantom's base Charles roared over Balmoral at over a thousand miles per hour, shattering the peace of the family's summer afternoon and qualifying himself as a member of the exclusive Ten Ton Club.

He also flew in an anti-submarine Nimrod during a day-long sortie over the Atlantic and later took part in a high-level 'bombing' attack on board a Vulcan nuclear bomber, in which he scored a 'direct hit' on a target in Doncaster.

He still found time to enjoy his favourite occupations, in spite of the intensity of the course. He would occasionally slip away to Sandringham for weekends or explore the countryside around Cranwell in the blue Aston Martin which had replaced his MGB. Disguised in the relative anonymity of his RAF uniform, he could wander round old churches and historic buildings without arousing curiosity or unwanted attention. He even found time to organize a Goonish practical joke on April Fool's Day, when he had a bogus announcement made over the public-address system which informed his fellow-officers that a manufacturer of their shoes had discovered a fault in the heels and that all officers were requested to bring their shoes to the porter's lodge. A good many of his fellow cadets had Flight-Lieutenant the Prince of Wales to thank when they found themselves barefoot and embarrassed after the hoax was revealed a few hours later.

The five-month course was almost over when Charles dropped a major bombshell. He wanted to make a parachute jump like all the other cadets. This sent ripples of anxiety running through all the top-brass in the Air Force and the Ministry of Defence, and was the sort of 'royal first' the Queen could well have done without. However, her son was not to be dissuaded. Perhaps he felt that he had been mollycoddled enough as 'Golden Eagle' and wanted to prove to himself and to the others that he was really worthy of his wings. Perhaps it was simply a case of being 'stupid enough to like trying things'. As he once said, 'I like to see if I can challenge myself to do something that is potentially hazardous, just to see if mentally I can accept that challenge and carry it out.' Whatever his reasons, his wishes prevailed against more sober counsels, and he found himself undergoing a course of parachute-training at RAF Abingdon, near Oxford, prior to jumping into the English Channel on the evening of 28 July 1971.

Twelve hundred feet above Studland Bay, on the Dorset coast, Charles waited apprehensively for his turn to jump. He had watched two senior officers disappear out of the doorway before him. He had checked his emergency parachute attached to the front of his harness. Now he was waiting, with butterflies in his stomach, for the green light and the tap on his shoulder from the flight sergeant who was there to 'help' him out. The light shone green, he felt the tap and jumped without hesitation. As soon as he was out of the aircraft, he realized that something had gone wrong. Describing the experience afterwards, his cheerful nonchalance glossed over what must have been a hair-raising experience:

Out I went ... the slip-stream is terrific. You appear to be flipped on your back, and the next thing I knew my feet were above my head caught in the rigging lines, very odd. I thought, 'They didn't tell me anything about this.' Fortunately my feet weren't twisted around the lines and came out very quickly. The Royal Marines were roaring around in little rubber boats underneath, and I was out of the water in ten seconds. A hairy experience.

Charles passed out from Cranwell three weeks later, on 20 August 1971. His report stated that he would 'make an excellent fighter pilot at supersonic speeds'. It went on to commend his natural flying ability and his skill at performing aerobatics in jets.

Charles could not conceal his obvious happiness and delight as he received his wings from Air Chief Marshall Sir Denis Spotswood, while the band played 'God Bless the Prince of Wales'. Standing in the crowd of spectators, wearing his uniform

20 August 1971, A proud Prince Philip with his son at the 'Wings' ceremony at Cranwell. The report on Prince Charles stated he was a pilot of 'particular flying abilities'.

of Marshall of the Royal Air Force, was his father, who fourteen years before had bellowed encouragement to the eight-year-old commander of the Hill House gun-crew. Now he could pose for photographs with a mature, self-assured and supremely successful officer in the RAF. Prince Philip was clearly 'tickled pink' by Charles's performance, and although he declined to shake hands with his son for the benefit of the Press, he showed his obvious pleasure at the occasion by remarking, 'I'll stand on my head if you like.'

The proud parent must have been just as pleased with the next phase of his son's career, his five years of service in the Royal Navy. Apart from Prince Philip's own love of the sea and the naval life which he had been forced to renounce at an early age because of his father-in-law's ill-health, he saw a naval career as an invaluable training for Charles. 'Going to sea is not purely a military operation,' he explained, 'it is a professional one. Altogether you live in a highly technological atmosphere, probably a good introduction to the kind of thing that controls our whole existence. And aboard ship you learn to live with people, that is the important thing.'

Charles would not be simply following his father's footsteps though. He would be the most recent in a line of royal sailors that stretched back to King George V, his great-grandfather. His grandfather, King George VI, had not distinguished himself at Dartmouth, but he had seen active service in the battle of Jutland in 1916. The most celebrated naval figure in the family was Charles's great-uncle, Earl Mountbatten. He had been the heroic commander of the beleaguered HMS *Kelly* during the war and later became First Sea Lord filling the office that his father, Prince Louis of Battenberg, had been forced to resign during the First World War because his German ancestry was considered to be against the interest of Britain while she was at war with Germany.

As in the RAF, Charles joined the navy as a graduate entrant and 'went aboard' the Royal Naval College at Dartmouth with a dozen other graduate officers to undergo the six-week course that quickly licks them into shape and makes them worthy of command.

During those six weeks the acting sub-lieutenants lived a non-stop twelve-hour day that started before seven each morning. The Prince and his classmates were subjected to daily sessions of square-bashing on the parade-ground under the critical eyes and constant haranguing of petty officers. 'We have no special attitude towards graduates,' said the officer in charge of putting them through their paces. 'They get kicked to death like any other man. But I think most people enjoy it. It can be fun.'

Other physical exertions included passing a standard swimming-test in a boiler-suit and undergoing exhausting routines in the gym. But the main part of the course was spent in the classrooms studying seamanship, navigation, engineering and essential management skills. Here again Charles had to struggle with his technical inadequacies. At the end of the course though, he came out top in navigation and seamanship, which, as his great-uncle commented, 'is all we care about'.

Charles's first ship was the guided-missile destroyer HMS *Norfolk*, which he joined in Gibraltar on 5 November 1971 – a 'fiendishly chosen date' as Charles observed. The ship was taking part in NATO exercises in the Mediterranean, and less than a fortnight after joining her, Charles was spending his twenty-third birthday as a second officer of the watch being buffeted by a force-ten gale off the coast of Sardinia. Other duties were concerned with his studies directed towards gaining his naval certificate of competence and a watch-keeping certificate, qualifying him to take complete charge of a ship as an Officer of the Watch.

After five weeks at sea, the *Norfolk* docked at Portsmouth for a few days' leave, which allowed the crew to spend Christmas with their families. Charles went to Windsor Castle and the rest of the crew dispersed to their own homes.

After the short Christmas break it was back to work and study. With the *Norfolk* stationed at Portsmouth, Charles attended courses at the shore base, *HMS Dryad*, where he studied bridgework, communications and gunnery. Problems arose however at another base, *HMS Dolphin*, where, as part of his basic submarine training, he was expected to practise emergency escapes without breathing apparatus.

There were many in the higher echelons of the admiralty who were unhappy at the idea of the Heir Apparent risking his life in a hundred-foot-high tank filled with seven hundred gallons of sea-water. Charles however was adamant that he should undergo the test like any other sub-lieutenant.

After the necessary instruction therefore, Charles found himself in the mock-up of the submarine air-lock protected only by goggles, a nose-clip and his wits. The door was shut behind him. The connecting door with the tank was then opened, and the water flooded in. As it rose above his shoulders, Charles took a deep breath and stepped into the base of the tank. The natural buoyancy of his body took him to the surface, but during the fifteen-second ascent he had to remember to breathe out, or 'whistle to the top' as the instructor had called it. Failure to do this could have resulted in permanent damage to his lungs or heart caused by the water-pressure.

After three weeks aboard the Fleet Air Arm frigate HMS *Hermione*, which was taking part in a mock attack on Portland, Charles returned to the *Norfolk* and more NATO exercises in the Mediterranean. This cruise established a pattern that would characterize most of his time in the Navy. As well as performing his duties as a serving officer, he was also called upon to take part in an increasing number of official royal duties. Charles was frequently to be found poring over state papers as well as those from his staff at Buckingham Palace and in the Duchy of Cornwall

Prince Charles inspecting a tank at close quarters during a visit to the Welsh Regiment at Osnabruck.

OPPOSITE *Prince Charles chats to soldiers of the Cheshire Regiment.*

ABOVE *Before taking a parachute jump.*

while his brother officers were enjoying their off-duty breaks.

Official visits also intruded into his naval life. While on board the *Norfolk*, he had to accompany the Queen on a two-day state visit to France, while the rest of the *Norfolk*'s crew were extending the *entente cordiale* in Toulon in the time-honoured naval manner. Less than a fortnight after rejoining 'the shop', Charles was called back home suddenly to attend the funeral of his great-uncle the Duke of Windsor, a former Prince of Wales.

The period between Prince Charles's leaving the *Norfolk* and joining his next ship, HMS *Minerva* (a Leander class frigate), was filled with the same combination of Service and official duties. There were courses on signals at HMS *Mercury* and further courses at HMS *Dryad* in which he was educated in the finer points of nuclear and biological warfare. Charles also went on a refresher course at Cranwell, during which he flew the Hunter jet fighter. A new dimension was added to his flying experience at the Royal Naval Air Base at Yeovilton in Somerset, where Charles was introduced to helicopter flying for the first time.

The other side of his life saw him paying an official visit to West Germany to attend training-exercises of the Prince of Wales Division, as well as fitting in a private shooting-trip to the Duke of Wellington's Spanish estate. He spent his twenty-fourth birthday at home and six days later joined his sister in hosting a private dinner-party to celebrate their parents' twenty-fifth wedding anniversary.

This happy event was barely over when Charles was off to sea again, this time as one of the seventeen officers on board HMS *Minerva*.

As a general-purpose ship, the *Minerva* was ideally suited to Charles's dual rôle as officer and royal ambassador. When she sailed away for a six-month cruise of the Caribbean, he was well briefed on all the official visits he was due to make in the West Indies. Once again, while the other members of the crew relaxed, the Prince worked. The ship's company was received with lavish hospitality in every port of call, but although the entertainments had been laid on principally to honour the Prince of Wales he was seldom free to join in with the same abandon as his shipmates.

When *Minerva* docked in Bermuda, Charles went to meet the Governor, Sir Richard Sharples. Only a week after the Prince's visit, the Governor and a young aide were assassinated while walking the path Sir Richard had taken with the Prince. Many people thought that the young aide had been mistaken for Charles, but whether this was the case or not, their murder was a salutary warning to all concerned with the Prince's security.

After a brief return home to join in the celebrations of his sister's engagement to Lieutenant Mark Phillips, Charles returned to his ship as a lieutenant himself. His new rank brought with it responsibility for the ship's 45-inch guns and her deployment of Seacat missiles. Another of his duties was the supervision of the band, which was to play at the independence celebrations of the Bahamas, at which Charles would represent the Queen.

The festivities surrounding the independence celebrations were boisterous and exotic in true Caribbean style, and right in the thick of the carnival atmosphere was Lieutenant HRH the Prince of Wales, joining in the energetic local dancing and encouraging the rest of the crew to join in the fun.

'At sea you learn to live with people,' Prince Philip had told Charles, and the wisdom of this advice became apparent during the rest of his cruise on HMS *Minerva*. In the long weeks at sea Charles was free for a time from official papers, royal correspondence, personal body-guards and the Press. As an officer he was responsible for the welfare of the men under his command, which meant taking an active interest in their lives at home as well as at sea. He was expected to listen to their problems with wives or girl-friends and generally to act as a counsellor to any member of the crew. At the same time, he was asked familiar questions about his family life in Buckingham Palace. In the confined world of the ship he learned to speak more informally and openly about himself and his home. He also learned the value of trust among friends. Little, if anything, of those intimate chats was ever divulged to the world at large.

Charles undertook his first prolonged period of royal duties after he left the *Minerva* in September 1973. For part of that time he acted as Senior Counsellor of

OPPOSITE *Like his father and great-uncle Charles greatly enjoyed his time in the Navy and proved himself an able and conscientious sailor. Here he relaxes in naval uniform.*

State while the Queen was away in Australia, and for the first time he received new ambassadors when they came to present their credentials at the Court of St James's. He also attended the State Opening of Parliament and wore his naval uniform in public for the first time. He began to experience the tight schedules that would increasingly control his life – one morning he flew to Luxembourg to attend a conference and was back in London the same evening to attend a charity fund-raising reception.

The break between ships also allowed him the chance to spend some time in his Principality and in the Duchy of Cornwall, where he spoke at public gatherings and enjoyed more informal gatherings with groups of his tenants.

The climax of those four months came on 14 November, not with his own twenty-fifth birthday but with his sister's wedding to the recently promoted Captain Phillips. Anne's wedding started rumours flying yet again about Charles's own marriage plans, but, as before and since, these were hastily scotched by the Prince.

On the second day of 1974 Charles flew to Singapore to join HMS *Jupiter*, also a Leander class frigate, as communications officer on a cruise in the Far East, which was to take him back to his 'second home', Australia. On that occasion though, New Zealand must have seemed even more like home, when his family gathered in Christchurch for the Commonwealth Games at the beginning of February. *Jupiter* docked in Christchurch at dawn on 29 January only six berths away from *Britannia*, in which Prince Philip was doubtless still peacefully asleep. Anyone watching the incoming ship after she had made fast would have noticed a young naval officer darting along the dock towards the royal yacht. Charles was eager to be the first to wake his father that morning. His mother, sister and brother-in-law joined the two of them the following day.

After attending the Games, Charles left the other members of the Royal Family and rejoined his ship to continue her voyage to California, calling at a number of islands on the way. After a stop-over at San Diego, the *Jupiter* started for home on her long voyage back through the Panama Canal and across the Atlantic, and the communications officer started to become acquainted with naval helicopters as part of his duties. On the ship he was concerned only with supervising the landing and take-off of the Wasp anti-submarine helicopter. Watching the aircraft soaring away from the deck and disappearing into the horizon, however, fired his imagination and re-kindled his love of flying. So, by the time the *Jupiter* returned to her home port after her round-the-world cruise, 'Taffy Windsor', as the crew affectionately referred to the Heir Apparent, had set his sights on mastering those difficult and challenging aircraft. As Prince Philip had gained his helicopter's pilot's licence when he was thirty-five, Charles was eager to get his ten years earlier. For a man with a flair for living dangerously, flying helicopters was an exciting challenge.

During the course of the *Jupiter*'s voyage, Charles's fellow-officers had occasionally allowed their deference to him to lapse to the point when he had to jokingly remind them of who he was. He used to threaten them with being sent to the Tower after some of these playful affronts, adding, 'I can, you know. It's quite within my right.' Sure enough, when the *Jupiter* docked at Plymouth, there was a black minibus waiting on the quay emblazoned with the sign in gold letters 'HMS *Tower of London* for officers of HMS *Jupiter*'.

Unfortunately not all the assaults on his dignity and position were as humorous as those on the ship, as Charles became only too aware. He was attending a course on underwater warfare at Portland and was being accommodated in shore barracks when the one serious attack on his life was made.

He was woken by a sound in the room next to his bedroom at about two o'clock one morning. When he opened the door to see what was going on, someone rushed at him out of the darkness. The noise of fighting and struggling woke Charles's detective, Chief Inspector Paul Officer, who burst into the room just in time to prevent the assailant from bringing a chair down across the Prince's head. Between them, Officer and Charles overpowered the attacker, who was quickly hustled away by naval police. He turned out to be a naval lieutenant who had a history of mental instability and had just had a brainstorm. He was subsequently committed to a

Prince Charles has visited Canada many times. In 1975 his trip included a visit to the arctic wastes of the Northern Territories.

In the rugged Canadian surroundings Charles had the opportunity to pit himself against new challenges, such as diving into the freezing arctic waters (opposite).

naval hospital. Luckily Charles suffered only slight bruising, but both he and his security staff knew that he had had a lucky escape. In future, security both at sea and on shore was tightened considerably.

After that disturbing event, it was a happy coincidence that the most enjoyable time he was to spend in the services should follow so soon afterwards. During the three-month helicopter-training course at Yeovilton, Charles was to find his true métier in the services, a combination of life at sea and his love of flying.

Once again, this course, like all the others, had to be condensed into a tight programme, and in spite of his previous flying experience Charles soon learned that helicopters were every bit as difficult to fly as he had hoped.

As part of the aptly named Red Dragon flight, Charles was taught to fly one of the most testing of those demanding aircraft, the large twin-engined Wessex commando helicopter. At Yeovilton he learned to fly the Wessex in all weather conditions and over both land and sea. Flying in the rugged mountains of North Wales, he landed on the summit of Snowdon, while over the sea he learned to hover just above the waves, while practising air-sea rescue. He learned the value of the safety procedures he had practised time and again on the ground, when on one occasion one of his engines caught fire and he was forced to make an emergency landing in a field.

Apart from reconnaisance work and firing rockets or guided missiles, naval helicopters perform the important task of carrying commandos into battle. So Charles and the other pilots on his course were sent on a commando training-exercise to have a taste of what their 'passengers' had to go through. At the Royal Marines training-centre at Lympstone in Devon, Charles was put through his paces over a gruelling assault-course. Above the ground he had to 'swing over chasms on ropes, slide down ropes at death-defying speed and then walk across wires strung between a pole and a tree', while below ground he was made to crawl through a series of tunnels half-filled with water, finishing off with one that was completely full. After the ordeal was over, the Marines' only comment was that the Prince had shown that he was reasonably fit.

Even during this spell of intensive training at Yeovilton, Charles was called away to the other side of the world on two occasions. The first was a lightning visit to New Zealand for the funeral of the late Prime Minister, Sir Robert Menzies. The second was a three-week tour of Fiji and Australia in October. During the visit to Fiji he represented the Queen at the centenary celebrations of the country's association with Britain. He received an ecstatic reception from both young and old. He danced with garlanded girls, and was even ensnared by one particularly alluring partner into the local love-dance. He was also able to meet twelve descendants of the native chiefs who had originally ceded Fiji to his great-great-great-grandmother, Victoria, one hundred years before.

His visit to Australia had been intended primarily to open the huge Anglo-Australian telescope in New South Wales. However, Charles took the opportunity while he was there of meeting up with some of his old friends from Timbertop, and in Tasmania he came across another figure from school days, Philip Beck, son of his former headmaster at Cheam. 'I remember your father well,' Charles told Beck. 'He caned me once – no, twice. The hidings were for ragging.'

In spite of these interruptions, he still had to keep up the tight schedule of his helicopter training when he was in England, and after 105 hours flying, which had been compressed into only forty-five days, he went solo for the first time and became an operational combat pilot. When the course ended, on 1 December 1974, Charles was awarded the double diamond trophy for the pilot who had made the most progress. The pilot's own summary of the three months was, 'very exciting, very rewarding, very stimulating and sometimes bloody terrifying'. Apart from this success, the months at Yeovilton had galvanized his principal interests in the Services. He knew now that his ideal branch of the armed forces would be the Fleet Air Arm. As he revealed later in a foreword to a history of the Fleet Air Arm, this had a particularly family significance for him. 'Pride swells in my heart,' he wrote, 'when I consider the part played by my great-grandfather, Prince Louis of Battenberg, in the formation of the Royal Naval Air Squadron in 1914. Without his interest and enthusiasm and his determined support of the aeroplane versus the airship, the Naval Air Service might quite literally have had difficulty in getting off the ground.'

Indeed it was Charles's own unbounded enthusiasm for the Fleet Air Arm that dictated his next posting to the commando-carrier HMS Hermes. With Red Dragon flight he joined the ship as a front-line operational unit and sailed across the Atlantic to join NATO exercises.

It is a credit to the Ministry of Defence that they allowed the Heir Apparent to take part in what amounted to some of the most testing and hazardous aspects of

Despite his official position, Charles has never shied from taking his full share of the rigours of life aboard ship.

modern warfare. Charles was well aware of the risks involved in flying helicopters in conditions as varied as the sub-tropical forests of the Caribbean and the Arctic wastes of northern Canada. He also appreciated the even greater risks taken by others, risks that he knew would never be open to him.

I adore flying [he told one interviewer], and I personally can't think of a better combination than naval flying – being at sea and being able to fly . . . I think that people who fly in the Fleet Air Arm are of a very high standard, particularly those chaps who fly Buccaneers and Phantoms. These people are taking all kinds of risks. Taking off and landing on carriers, particularly at night, is no joke at all. If you're living dangerously, it tends to make you appreciate life that much more and to really want to live it to its fullest. They're some of the most invigorating and amusing people that I've come across.

He went on an official tour of northern Canada only a few weeks after joining the *Hermes* and used that visit to the frozen north as an opportunity to have a taste of Eskimo life – and of the less enthralling Eskimo food. He also undertook one of the most hazardous royal visits ever made while he was there, diving beneath the ice-cap to look at life in the frozen Arctic waters.

The occasion of this unprecedented royal feat was a visit to the headquarters of a marine research unit in Resolute Bay. The director of the unit was a Dr Joe MacInnis, with whom Charles disappeared through a hole in the six-feet-thick ice to

ABOVE LEFT *Taking part in a tough commando assault course.*

ABOVE RIGHT *15 December 1976. Prince Charles is wheeled off his ship* HMS Bronington *at the end of his naval career.*

RIGHT *Sporting a 'full set'.*

slip into the icy green water beneath. Although Charles had trained as a naval frogman, he had never experienced conditions like those before. The water-temperature was 28.5 degrees Fahrenheit. In that incredibly cold water one slit in his specially heated wet-suit would mean death in a minute. Naturally Charles's security staff had their hearts in their mouths during the half-hour dive. But Charles characteristically soon overcame any anxiety he might have felt and became engrossed in the strange world beneath the ice. 'It was a fascinating eerie world of greyish-green light that met my gaze, and above all was the roof of ice which disappeared into the distance,' was the way he later described it.

Once he had got used to the strange wet-suit and the bitter cold around his mouth and the extremities of his body, Charles started to enjoy himself. Guided by Dr MacInnis, he floated up to the bottom of the ice feet-first to try walking upside down like a fly on a ceiling. After only partial success at this game, he descended to the sea-bed laboratory to look at the Canadian scientist's experiments.

By the time he came back to the surface, Charles had been under the freezing water for thirty minutes. Even though a team of safety divers had been standing by, ready to plunge in at the slightest sign of an emergency, the security staff were extremely uneasy. It was Charles who, not for the first time, broke the tension by appearing outside the tent covering the hole in the ice looking like a grotesque orange 'Michelin man'. He had inflated his rubber diving-suit for the amusement of the Press corps. As a finale he opened the valve and allowed the suit to deflate, bowing to the delighted cameramen, while the rotund figure gradually sagged to look like a flabby 'orange walrus'.

His relations with the Press had come a long way from the irritation and intrusion he had experienced at school. In the gruelling tour of Canada a mutual admiration developed between the Press corps and the subject of their interest as both sides grew to appreciate the difficulties of the other's job in the wild, inhospitable surroundings. The pressmen composed a witty song as a form of jovial complaint about having to follow the Prince at break-neck speed across the Frozen North. Not to be outdone, Charles retaliated the next day with equally amusing lyrics, which he sang with his equerry, secretary and detective to the melody of the Welsh hymn *Immortal, Invisible, God only Wise*:

Impossible, unapproachable, God only knows
The light's always dreadful and he won't damn-well pose,
Most maddening, most curious, he simply can't fail,
It's always the same with the old Prince of Wales.

Insistent, persistent, the Press never end,
One day they will drive me right round the bend,
Recording, rephrasing, every word that I say,
It's got to be news by the end of the day.

A rather formal pose of Prince Charles in his Commander's uniform.

Disgraceful, most dangerous to share the same plane,
Denies me the chance to scratch and complain,
Oh where may I ask you is the monarchy going,
When Princes and pressmen are on the same Boeing?

The programme so formal and highly arranged,
But haven't you heard that it's all been changed,
Friday is Sunday and that is quite plain,
So no one, please no one, is allowed to complain.

When Charles returned to *Hermes*, she sailed to eastern Canada, where the Red Dragon flight joined their Canadian counterparts training at their base at Blissville, New Brunswick. Immediately after returning from a fortnight of arduous training, Charles flew back to London to be installed as a Knight of the Bath. This was singularly appropriate in view of the fact that he had been living in fairly cramped conditions under canvas for two weeks. When he flew into Heathrow, he was sporting a magnificent beard and moustache, which he had grown during the recent exercises. It was apparent, however, that the Queen did not share his son's enthusiasm for his recently acquired facial foliage. In fact, when he was installed by her in Henry VII's chapel in Westminster Abbey the following morning, the beard had disappeared, and the moustache had gone too when he flew back to join his ship the next day. In the Abbey Charles had been dressed as a Colonel of the Welsh Guards, and as such he was permitted to wear just a moustache like any other army officer. When he reverted to being a naval officer the next day, he was again subject to naval regulations that stipulate that a full set of beard and moustache must be worn or nothing at all.

The spell of duty on HMS *Hermes*, which ended in the summer of 1975, had marked the climax of Charles's experience as a front-line officer. He had proved himself capable of flying in any weather and in any part of the world. He had formed part of one of the most highly trained units in the armed forces. The great enjoyment which he found in serving on board the ship is aptly expressed in the yellow T-shirt that he proudly sports bearing the unequivocal motif 'Happy Hermes'.

The final phase of Earl Mountbatten's master-plan for his great nephew was a spell at sea with a command of his own. In the new year of 1976 Charles completed his captaincy course at Greenwich and Dartmouth and on 9 February, aged twenty-seven, he took command of the minesweeper HMS *Bronington*, which was based at Rosyth. When his father had been given command of HMS *Magpie* in 1950 he had been twenty-nine.

HMS *Bronington* is aptly named after a village in Wales. Wooden-hulled and weighing only 360 tons she is one of the oldest and smallest ships in the Royal Navy, and during his ten months in her command, *Bronington* was involved in a variety of duties at sea. On one occasion she had to shadow a Russian submarine caught prowling off the coast. Throughout his time on board Charles was kept busy putting into practice the theory he had learned during the previous five years. He was kept busy in other ways too: the out-going captain had warned him that the *Bronington* 'rolled on wet grass', and Charles quickly found out that she was the only ship to make him seasick in all his time in the navy. Putting into Rosyth after his first ten weeks with her at sea, the new captain commented that it had 'taken ten years off my life. . . . I feel about eighty'.

Like his father's before him, Charles's period of command was brought to an end by the demands of royal duty. A month after his twenty-eighth birthday he was gazetted a Wing Commander in the RAF and a Commander in the Royal Navy, jumping the rank of Lieutenant-Commander in the process. The following day he left the Services to return to life as a civilian.

The small intimate crew of the *Bronington* showed their affection for their popular and respected skipper in true naval tradition. They pushed him ashore in a wheelchair, garlanded with a black lavatory-seat inscribed with the ship's name in gold letters. This was to remind him of the responsibilities of the throne. Not that he would need any reminding. Twenty-four years of training were over. The job was about to begin in earnest.

7

The Working Prince

1977, the year of the Queen's Silver Jubilee, was a significant year in the life of her eldest son as well. He had completed his grooming for kingship as prescribed by his great-uncle, and was now ready to begin his work as Prince of Wales.

But what exactly was there for him to do? His two immediate predecessors as Prince of Wales, the future Edward VII and Edward VIII, had been given no clear rôle, and neither had proved a favourable example for a modern Prince of Wales to follow. Although it was highly unlikely that Charles would ever behave with the same carefree abandon as his predecessors, it was very important that he should be occupied and, furthermore, under the eagle eye of monarchy-knocking MP Willie Hamilton and his supporters, that he should be *seen* to be occupied.

One of the few advantageous precedents set by Edward VIII was the part he had played in his father's Silver Jubilee celebrations in 1935. As Prince of Wales he had launched a fund-raising campaign under the simple slogan 'For Youth'. In spite of the Depression, that appeal had been tremendously successful, and the fund was still in existence in 1977 as the King George V Jubilee Trust. It seemed highly appropriate therefore that forty-two years later George V's great-grandson should undertake a similar responsibility for the young people of his own generation during his mother's Silver Jubilee Year. This would be his first major national initiative and a blueprint for his work in the future.

Apart from the happy coincidence, the idea was well suited to Charles's own interests. Long before plans for the Jubilee Appeal were laid down, he had been actively engaged in working for and with young people. Three years before leaving the Navy, Charles had started chairing an invited committee of social-workers, welfare-officers and police representatives, in an attempt to find a way of diverting underprivileged children away from a life of monotony and boredom that leads frequently to delinquency and crime.

Although Charles's ideas, like those of his father, clearly reflected the spartan philosophy of the educationalist Kurt Hahn, he was open to suggestion from those experienced in dealing with children from deprived backgrounds. The committee quickly decided therefore that any scheme it evolved should concentrate on helping

OPPOSITE *Having planted a tree to commemorate his tour of the West Coast of Africa the Prince is handed a watering can so that he can finish the job off properly.*

young people who feel aimless, unlike the Duke of Edinburgh's Award Scheme which aims to inspire those who are already strongly motivated to achieve success and which Charles had participated in while at Gordonstoun. Most of the applications for grants were channelled through the police and welfare services. Specific groups of young people in different areas of the country who had come to the attention of the police were offered funds to begin some sort of community or self-help project.

Charles was away at sea for much of the time and chose to keep a very low profile as the scheme got off the ground. But after nearly three years, word began to get around that he had been instrumental in bringing help to the groups who had received grants. The steady flow of project reports and accounts of the use to which the money had been put immediately swelled to an avalanche of mail thanking the Prince. It was clear that the time had come for the scheme to be developed into a charitable trust, and in 1976 the Queen gave her permission for it to be called 'The Prince's Trust'. Formally established, it set itself a suitably formal and lofty aim: 'To enable young people to find adventure, excitement and achievement by carrying through their own enterprises, which contribute to their own or other people's development.'

By the time the Silver Jubilee Appeal was launched, the Prince's Trust had been in existence for a year, and Charles had four years' experience of youth work to look back on. Even so, there were many people who heard his launching speech on 24 April 1977 with some misgivings. Appeals to the rugged life of the great outdoors, coupled with concepts of duty and ideals of public service, bore the unmistakeable stamp of Gordonstoun and sounded far removed from the lives of most of the people listening to the speech. But there could be no denying Charles's obvious commitment to the campaign or the sincerity of his address, despite what many mistook to be his social naïveté.

There were many who saw significance in the fact that the speech was made from what was then his official residence, Chevening in Kent. This seemed to indicate a new phase in his career as a full-time Prince of Wales with no more military commitments. Interestingly, although the eighty-three-roomed stately home was given to the nation by the late Lord Stanhope with the specific request that it be used as the official residence of all future Princes of Wales, Charles never really took to the house. In 1980 he gave it up and bought Highgrove, near Tetbury in the Cotswolds, which is much closer to one of his major concerns, the Duchy of Cornwall. In his Chevening speech, Charles was careful to point out that the Silver Jubilee Appeal was very much a family initiative:

I felt it would be marvellous if there was some permanent way in which we could mark the twenty-five years of service which the Queen has given to the country and the Commonwealth. So I asked my mother what she would like us to do. After careful consideration she said she would be particularly pleased if money could be raised principally to assist and encourage the outstanding work already being done by young people in various fields.

A little over a year after speaking to the nation from Chevening, Charles was able proudly to announce from Buckingham Palace that the Appeal had raised over £16 million. It was clear that, far from being a possible deterrent, Charles's association with the Appeal had been a major incentive.

Raising the money was only the beginning of the project, though, as is often the case, it was the aspect that received the greatest attention. The work of putting the money to good use then had to start. First the existing King George V Jubilee Trust was amalgamated with the recently raised money to form 'The Royal Jubilee Trusts'. As Chairman of the Trusts, Charles takes a close interest in the appeals for grants and in the way the money is allocated. Not content with sitting behind a desk master-minding the allocation of grants, he makes a point of visiting groups that have received aid, wherever he is visiting, no matter how tight his schedule.

Another example of his involvement in more than just name was his patronage of the two-year round-the-world expedition 'Operation Drake', in which different crews of young people aged under twenty-five sailed a 150-ton brigantine following Drake's original route round the world. Here again the adventurous Prince seemed to be an ideal patron. Not content to be a patron only in name, he was determined to

*The Queen's Silver Jubilee of 1977 marked the beginning of a new phase
in Prince Charles's career . . .*

... in which he began work as a full-time member of the family 'firm'. His many years of training had prepared him well ...

play a positive part in the expedition as well. He therefore sponsored one of the two hundred participants and donated nearly half the sum needed to replace the ship's engine. Speaking to the first of the crews as they were about to depart for two weeks' sea-trials, he told them: 'I expect there will be moments when you wish you were back home, wish you had never volunteered in the first place, but my advice to you is "Stick to it".' When the expedition returned in December 1980 Prince Charles visited the exhibition set up at St Katharine's Dock to record the exploits of the young explorers and was able to chat to them about their experiences.

He was also a natural choice as patron for the ambitious three-year Transglobe Expedition that set out in September 1979 to traverse the world by passing through both poles. He realized the importance of such an expedition to British exports in a wide range of products, another of his leading interests and concerns. Much of the equipment for the polar regions must have been familiar to Charles after his experiences in northern Canada, and the eagerness with which he examined the exhibits at the launching ceremony would have made one think that he was part of the team.

It must be very hard on an active, intelligent young man, who by his own admission has learned the thrill of living dangerously, to see others setting off on trips of a lifetime that he knows full well he will never be able to undertake himself. His grandmother once said that if there was anything left to discover in the world, Charles would probably have been an explorer, and this is backed up by the intense

... and the once shy Prince is never at a loss for conversation. Like his father, he has the knack of putting everyone he meets at their ease.

and wide-ranging interest he shows in any form of adventure or exploration.

However, the Prince's patronage extends far beyond adventurous expeditions. It includes organizations as far apart as the Somerset County Federation of Young Farmers, the Friends of Brecon Cathedral and the British Surfing Association.

He has always been generous with the time he has devoted to his patronages. He has taken part in a film made to raise money for the Royal Opera House, Covent Garden, in which he was delighted to be filmed conducting the orchestra during a rehearsal for Mozart's *Magic Flute*. Although he openly admits his ignorance of opera, he is equally frank about his eagerness to get to know more about it. One of the perquisites of being a patron of Covent Garden is that he can visit it whenever he chooses, and he seldom misses an opportunity to slip into the royal box to hear an unknown work or listen to an old favourite. For their first night out together in public Prince Charles and Lady Diana Spencer went to Covent Garden to see the American soprano Grace Bumbry in Meyerbeer's opera *L'Africaine*. A week later their first public engagement together was at a recital at Goldsmith's Hall put on to raise money for a new extension to the Royal Opera House.

A typical example of his diligence as a patron is his involvement with the Royal Anthropological Institute. He took over the position following the tragic death of his cousin Prince William of Gloucester in a flying accident in 1972. His study of the subject at Cambridge fired his keenness for the new responsibility, and he threw himself into the job with characteristic enthusiasm and matter-of-fact application.

Prince Charles, Prince Philip and the Duke of Kent ride behind the Queen during the Trooping of the Colour ceremony.

Looking at the work of the Institute in a practical sense, he remarked in an interview:

> What attracts me is that, the stronger and more widely influential the Anthropological Institute could be, the better contribution it could make to Britain in facing the problems of a multi-racial society. The more people understand about the background of immigrants who come to this country, the less apprehensive they would be about them. To get on neighbourly terms with people of other races and countries, you've got to get more familiar with them – know how they live, how they eat, how they work, what makes them laugh ... you can't change people's apprehensions in one night, but you can make a start by making them more knowledgeable. If the Anthropological Institute can help do that, I'm going to help.

True to his word, Charles did indeed help. With all the other demands on his time, he still managed to find time to present a seven-part series for the BBC under the title *Face Values*, which examined the social values and different ways of life of seven ethnic groups throughout the world.

In his introduction to the series Charles modestly explained his own involvement: 'I thought the best contribution I could make was to put the questions that the layman would ask experts.' The result was just that. The Prince's easy manner and engaging interest succeeded in extracting coherent answers from high-powered anthropologists, who are not always noted for lucid explanations of their work to the ordinary man in the street.

One of the foremost duties in the Prince's mind is his commitment to Wales.

Shortly after the assassination of Lord Mountbatten, the Prince makes a surprise visit to British soldiers on patrol in Northern Ireland.

Unlike his immediate predecessor, who once lamely remarked on a visit to the mining valleys to see the lines of unemployed during the Depression, 'Something must be done,' Charles not only makes sure that things are done but frequently does them himself. He has worked tirelessly to promote Welsh industry and boost tourism in the Principality. As Chairman of the Welsh Countryside Committee, he is passionately involved in efforts to protect the rugged beauty of Wales. 'I want as many people as possible in Wales to show they love their country as much as they say and sing they do,' he challenged his subjects in a cry for action which was worthy of Llewelyn himself.

Although many Welsh societies and organizations feature prominently in his portfolio of interests, the ones that hold the greatest significance in his eyes are probably those with military connections. Charles in fact chose to be invested Prince of Wales dressed in the ceremonial uniform of the recently formed Royal Regiment of Wales, of which he was made Colonel-in-Chief in 1969; when he rides with his mother for the Trooping of the Colour every June, he wears the uniform of a Colonel of the Welsh Guards. Like his father, he looks magnificent in the ceremonial uniforms he frequently wears in public, but he is equally at home in the combat clothes he wears on exercises and active service.

Many a squaddie must have been impressed and not a little encouraged by the sight of the slightly built heir to the throne tackling obstacle-courses which would have made him flinch himself. But if Charles wins their admiration and respect by his physical fitness and military expertise, he wins their affection and loyalty by his obvious compassion and consideration for others.

Less than three months after his life-long friend and genial mentor, Earl Mountbatten, had been murdered by a terrorist bomb in the Republic of Ireland, Charles persuaded the Queen and the Prime Minister to allow him to visit some of the British troops stationed in Ulster. Dressed like them in camouflaged combat-gear and surrounded by armed escorts, Charles went to see three of the regiments of which he was Colonel-in-Chief who were serving in the notorious 'bandit country' near the border. In spite of the intense security and the obvious danger, Charles was relaxed and cheerful as he chatted amiably with the officers and men. He visited the 2nd Battalion Parachute Regiment, which had lost sixteen of its number in a bomb attack and ambush at Warren Point, on the same day that Earl Mountbatten had been murdered. He also made an unannounced visit, by helicopter, to the Welsh Guards, who had lost a comrade, killed by a bomb, only a week before the Prince arrived.

Much of Charles's everyday work is concerned with the running of the Duchy of Cornwall, which is his only regular source of income, apart from his share of royal investments, for, unlike other members of the Royal Family, he does not receive any money from the government in the annual Civil List.

The Duchy dates back to 1337, when the title was created by Edward III and the tradition began of passing the title down to the eldest son of the reigning monarch. Today it comprises wealthy estates and properties that are situated mainly in the West Country. The total area amounts to about 130,000 acres and includes such disparate national landmarks as the Isles of Scilly, Dartmoor Prison and the Oval Cricket-Ground in Kennington. Agriculture plays an important part in the revenue from the Duchy, and the farming ranges from the harvesting of millions of oysters from the beds of the River Helford in Cornwall to the breeding of high-quality Devon Red Ruby cattle on the Prince's own 550-acre farm in east Cornwall.

Although the value of the Duchy has tactfully never been publicly calculated, the Prince of Wales must be one of the wealthiest land-owners in the country. In spite of being exempted from paying income tax, Charles nevertheless contributes half his annual profit, of about £250,000, to the Treasury as a form of income tax. Until he was eighteen almost all the income from the Duchy went to the Chancellor of the Exchequer, with the exception of sums retained by the Queen for her son's needs, £15,000 a year until his coming of age (at eighteen) and then double that amount until he was twenty-one.

Out of his income Charles has to pay the salaries of his staff at Buckingham Palace, Highgrove, and those employed by the Duchy. He has to buy his uniforms and clothes and to pay for the upkeep of his cars and sporting interests. In spite of these expenses, much of his money is ploughed back into the estates. The secretary to the Duchy once commented that,

The estates are not really run as profitably as they could be. What he takes out of the

March 1977. At the beginning of Silver Jubilee year the Prince paid official visits to Ghana and the Ivory Coast. He managed a very full schedule ...

Duchy is not much by today's standards, when you consider his expenses and the many donations he makes to charitable organizations.

He is hideously generous with his money and hardly ever ignores a request for help from an organization within the Duchy. He gives away an incredible amount of money.

In fact, while Charles was in the Services he never drew any pay from the RAF, and the salary he received from the Royal Navy was all donated to the King George V Mission to Seamen.

With such a sizeable enterprise, Charles cannot be expected to run the Duchy single-handed. In fact he acts as the managing director of an eight-man Prince's Council, which numbers some of the sharpest financial and estate-management brains in the country.

In view of Charles's constant public activity in Britain, it is often easy for us to forget that he plays an equally important part abroad. As he has often pointed out, his mother is just as much Queen of the Commonwealth as she is Queen of England, Scotland, Wales and Northern Ireland. It is therefore natural that her son should extend his interests at home into the broader field of international affairs. The Commonwealth plays a central part in this.

Charles is a great believer in the importance of the Commonwealth as one of the

. . . Over a million people turned out to greet him and many were given a personal wave or smile. For a short time Prince Charles assumed a different costume . . .

few international alliances with the potential for cutting through the divisions of race, colour, creed, language and wealth, that have seperated nations for so long. He told the audience at the Commonwealth Youth Conference in 1977 'I believe it is up to the young people of the Commonwealth to show that they believe that the association has something to offer the modern world, because without your support, interest and encouragement, it will be only a matter of time before the whole thing fades through lack of interest.'

This speech, made during the Silver Jubilee Year, coincided with the first year of major royal tours that Charles had yet undertaken. He had paid a few official visits around the world during his years in the navy, but 1977 was the first year in which they featured prominently in his annual programme.

Charles's tours are often proposed as much as eighteen months in advance. Once the go-ahead has been received from the Foreign Office, an advance-party visits the area of the tour. Nothing is left to chance: the route is inspected for security; guest lists are scrutinized; local diplomats are briefed on the protocol expected for the Prince of Wales. British diplomats are expected to provide information on sensitive political or social issues that should be avoided in conversation or speeches, because above all else Charles has to be seen as politically impartial in the internal politics of the countries he visits.

Care is taken for him to meet members of the resident British community and to

. . . and a different name, Nabu Charles Mampasa, when he was made an honorary chieftain. The tour was a huge success.

visit any British industrial or social interests in the country. Charles's personal likes and dislikes have to be taken into consideration as well. The possibility of snatching a game of polo, or going diving, opportunities to meet young people and the chance to greet old acquaintances all have to be borne in mind at the planning-stage.

The result is that, from the moment Charles steps on the plane at the start of the tour, both he and his staff know exactly what pattern the next few weeks will follow. Like an actor on stage, Charles comes over best when he is confident of the next cue and how he will respond to it. Even so, things do occasionally go wrong.

At the start of the tour of Ghana in March 1977, the first of Charles's Jubilee Year tours, his plane had to perform some minor aerobatics in order to avoid ploughing into the guard of honour, whose commander had absent-mindedly ordered his troops to march across the runway, right in front of the landing aircraft. As he inspected the troops a few minutes later, Charles could not avoid smiling to himself, though he spared the feelings of the unfortunate officer responsible.

He had the important job in Ghana of renewing old ties with the former colony, for he was the first royal visitor for sixteen years to set foot in the country. His official programme included meeting President Acheampong, who presented the Prince with a book of his best speeches! He attended celebrations of the fiftieth anniversary of the Achimoto School, in Accra, as well as visiting irrigation schemes and planting a tree to celebrate the Silver Jubilee. At other functions Charles posed in his military uniform with Ghanaian military cadets, and on another occasion he was dressed in the striped costume of a tribal chief and given the title of 'Naba Charles Mampasa'; throughout the rest of the tour, this new-found status entitled him to a raised seat, a 'medicine boy' and, perhaps more usefully, a parasol.

The highlight of the visit to Ghana was the *durbar* arranged to celebrate the Silver Jubilee. This was one of the very rare occasions when all the Ashanti chiefs gathered together, and it is done to honour only very high-ranking guests. The chiefs were dressed in an array of multi-coloured robes and festooned with gold bangles, rings and coronets – to the extent that one or two had to rest their hands on the shoulders of a boy walking in front to share the load on the arms. It was perfectly evident why Ghana had once been called 'the Gold Coast'.

Once the Jubilee celebrations were over at home, Charles was off again, this time travelling westwards to the Province of Alberta, in Canada, and more tribal rituals. On the second day of his five-day visit he flew deep into Indian territory to meet representatives of the Blackfoot tribe, who had signed a treaty with his great-great-great-grandmother a century before.

Not for the first time Charles found himself on the receiving end of a tirade of complaints about his mother's 'pale face' subjects. However Royal protocol prohibited him from expressing his own opinion and instead he had to respond with a few innocuous platitudes.

As a non-smoker Charles must have been relieved when the traditional peace-pipe rather ominously refused to smoke. But he willingly agreed to don the traditional costume of a tribal chief for the second time in four months. On this occasion it was not 'Naba Charles Mampasa' who appeared but 'Chief Red Crow' of the Kainai tribe. Complete with buckskins, feathered head-dress and war-paint, the new chief joined in the tribal dances in honour of the Sun, the Moon, the Grass and, inexplicably, the Chicken.

On the following day he swung to the other side of the western spectrum and appeared at the world-famous Calgary Rodeo. Dressed in full Wild West outfit of wide-brimmed stetson, smartly tailored cowboy-suit and leather boots, he greeted his brother Prince Andrew who had arrived from the Canadian school he was attending at the time, dressed in a similar outfit and looking like a matinée idol to the excited cowgirls who clustered around him. Both Princes were clearly the centre of attention, and they eagerly entered into the mood of the rodeo, so very different from the equestrian events they normally attend at home. Charles rode at the head of the five-mile-long procession that opened the rodeo, and as he passed his brother, watching from the raised stand, he made a low bow from the saddle. This was

OPPOSITE ABOVE *During his visit to Canada in 1977 Prince Charles was given the honorary title of Chief Red Crow.*

OPPOSITE BELOW *Wearing identical cowboy hats Prince Andrew and Prince Charles watch a rodeo together during a visit to Calgary, Canada.*

BELOW *The Prince meets Farrah Fawcett backstage at the London Palladium, after she compèred a show to raise funds for the United World Colleges, one of Lord Mountbatten's favourite causes.*

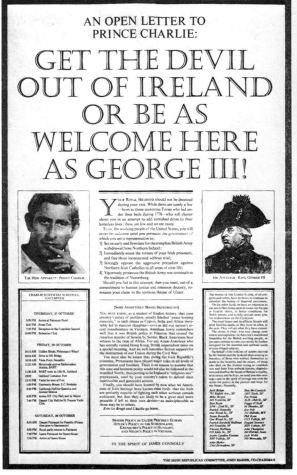

AN OPEN LETTER TO
PRINCE CHARLIE:

GET THE DEVIL OUT OF IRELAND OR BE AS WELCOME HERE AS GEORGE III!

THE IRISH REPUBLICAN COMMITTEE, JOHN MAHER, CO-CHAIRMAN

acknowledged by Andrew's raising his stetson in an equally flamboyant gesture. After the rodeo was over, Andrew went back to school while his elder brother had to fly home for more official duties, before returning to the New World in October to make a whistle-stop tour of twelve American cities in as many days.

The pace of that American visit put a terrific strain on Charles, although he always appeared composed and in good humour in spite of the pressure. Travelling over five thousand miles around the country meant that he was having to get up early and go to bed late, as well as suffering the added disadvantage of constantly crossing time-zones.

In Chicago he was mobbed by blue-rinsed matrons; in Texas he was nearly torn apart by the excited crowds, and in California he had to face small vociferous groups of IRA supporters who followed him around carrying miniature coffins.

Not all his encounters were so testing, for if that tour was outstanding for any one single factor it was the degree of feminine attention the Prince aroused. While in Hollywood he was the guest of honour at a charity dinner attended by some of the glossiest celebrities in that glossiest of all American towns. At dinner, Charles was

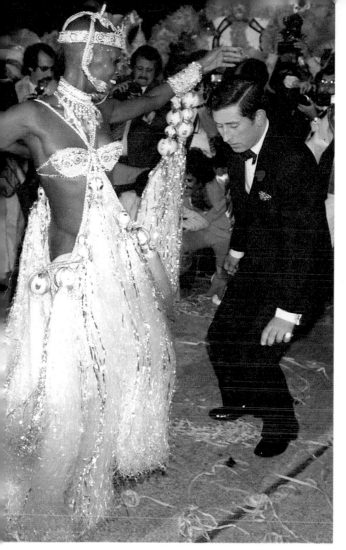

OPPOSITE *The Prince's tour of the United States led to several demonstrations and much criticism of the Royal Family and the British government from the many American supporters of the IRA. This newspaper advertisement is an example.*

LEFT *During a party given in his honour by the Mayor of Rio the Prince was persuaded to join in an energetic samba.*

flanked by two glamorous 'police' actresses, Angie Dickinson and Farrah Fawcett. 'I'm sitting between two of the most beautiful cops I've ever met,' he said in his speech of thanks for 'an amazingly enjoyable evening', and continued: 'I only wish I could arrange a swap with some of my policemen. I've been trying to persuade them to do that for years, but they won't agree.' Miss Dickinson was even more effusive in her praise of Charles: 'He's a beaut,' she confided to the attentive reporters, while Farrah Fawcett-Majors took it upon herself to overstep the bounds of decorum by patting the royal shoulder.

This admiration took on a more tangible form in the last city of Charles's tour, San Francisco. Having previously declined an invitation to the Hookers' Ball, which was being held to raise funds for the first prostitutes' union in the city, Charles did not show any objection to accepting a kiss from a more 'respectable' lady citizen, a soprano who had just been performing in a production of *Turandot* which the Prince had attended. By coincidence singer and Prince shared the same birthday, as she excitedly pointed out to him. However, this seemed to hold greater significance for the lady, who wistfully remarked, 'He's so eligible, and I'm so eligible.'

Although he doubtless found these encounters delightful and flattering, Charles aimed to leave a more substantial impression from his visit than that of playing Prince Charming for the benefit of starry-eyed American womanhood. Taking upon himself the often unenviable rôle of defender of his country overseas, he told an audience of fifteen hundred at a World's Fair Council lunch: 'Britain is an up-to-date society which is still in the forefront of technological and industrial advance, from nuclear power to Concorde'. He quoted surveys that showed that from the mid-1960s to the mid-1970s the number of days lost through strikes was on average lower in Britain than it had been in the USA. To drive his point home, he added that during a normal year ninety-eight per cent of the factories in Britain could expect to be strike-free.

By the time the tour of the USA had come to an end, Charles was exhausted. He admitted that he had been transformed from a live Prince into a semi-dead one. Before leaving, he confided to one of the Press corps: 'I have had my hand cut by ladies with long nails and shaken hands with so many people I need a hand transplant.' But instead of flying home to a well-earned rest, he flew west across the Pacific for yet another official visit, this time to Australia. This tour was just as demanding, with just as many girls eager to throw themselves at the Prince. Yet inevitably it was less of a strain, for Australia is very much the Prince's 'second home'.

1978 saw Charles's first official visit to Brazil and Venezuela. In Rio de Janeiro, his first port of call, he performed the usual rounds of visiting naval installations and factories, laying wreaths, giving Press conferences and visiting British residents. The event that excited the greatest attention was a party given by the Mayor of Rio in his honour. During the evening a party of samba dancers, dressed in outlandish carnival costumes, arrived to entertain the guests. Although he was more soberly dressed in a dinner-jacket, Charles could not resist the temptation to join in with them, and the next day newspapers throughout the world carried photographs of Charles dancing enthusiastically with a young Brazilian lady clad in little more than shredded tinfoil.

This South American tour emphasized one of the major frustrations of Charles's work and role, his inability to express his own point of view on social and political issues that interest and concern him. As an anthropologist he is interested in the Indian tribes of the Amazon jungles, and he can hardly have been unaware of the threat to their livelihood and environment presented by some of the policies of the present Brazilian government. In the same way, he could not have avoided reading about the claims of human-rights violations in the country. But these and topics like them are taboo subjects as far as Charles is concerned. He has to behave as if such issues did not exist. For a man committed to trying to understand the way different people live, such restrictions must seem infuriating most of the time.

Enforced political impotence also muted his response to his first view of life in a Communist country, when he visited Yugoslavia. Even though Yugoslavia practises a rather maverick form of Communism, Charles was still prohibited from uttering anything that might have been construed as a political point of view.

ABOVE LEFT *Prince Charles, piloting an Andover of the Queen's Flight, arrives in Yugoslavia.*

ABOVE RIGHT *The Prince's visit to Yugoslavia in October 1978 was his first to a Communist country. He is seen talking to President Tito.*

He had to content himself instead with having his finger bitten by a four-year old British tourist in Dubrovnik, viewing top-secret Yugoslav defence installations, visiting the sites of partisan resistance during the last war and lunching with President Tito. This last encounter might well have reminded Charles of his meeting with President Nixon eight years earlier. Both Tito and Nixon treated Charles to lengthy expositions of their view of the world order, and both of them must have been mildly surprised to discover that Charles did know something about international affairs and was quite capable of giving as good as he got, if not better. Following a visit to a naval base the next day, one senior Yugoslav official remarked that Charles's questions 'show that he knows more about Yugoslavia than we expected'. It was clear that few of his hosts realized that it is not uncommon for Charles to sit up until two o'clock in the morning when he is on tour, in order to familiarize himself with the next day's activities by doing as much background research as he can.

During 1979 Charles continued to develop into a seasoned campaigner. In the spring he spent six weeks in the Far East, Australia and Canada, the longest period in his 'working life' that he had been away from the UK. In November he flew to Asia once again, this time to make the long-awaited tour of India and Nepal, which had been cancelled four years previously due to the political unrest during the period of Emergency.

Since 1981 the unaffected charm and good looks of his wife have added immeasurably to the success of Prince Charles's official engagements, at home and abroad. Charles has shown a touching concern to steer his new Princess through the potential hazards of protocol, and, with her own determination to overcome her natural shyness, they have become a great popular success. The Working Princess has proved herself a perfect match for the Working Prince.

8

The Sporting Prince

One of the most marked differences between Prince Charles the boy and Prince Charles the man is the apparent change in his attitude to sport. The chubby, unenthusiastic schoolboy who showed little fondness for games at school has grown into an almost manically active adult, whose slim, athletic physique has changed little in the last ten years.

Charles could be mistaken by many for a fitness-fanatic. Most days begin with either a run or a swim, sometimes both if the opportunity presents itself. One day in Australia he woke his entourage before six in the morning so that they could all drive sixty miles for a dip before beginning the day's packed programme of engagements four hours later.

He does not smoke and drinks considerably less than most men of his age. Like his father, he never wastes a minute of his time in sitting around doing nothing. During the gruelling six weeks he spent at Dartmouth being 'kicked' into shape by the Royal Navy, his few hours of free time were spent either dinghy-sailing or playing squash. Even on holiday he is more often seen swimming or water-skiing then lying on the beach sunbathing. If the Gordonstoun motto 'There is more in you' can be said to influence any single aspect of his life, it is surely his attitude to sport.

That is not to say that his preference in sports has altered since his schooldays. It is noticeable that he still opts for those that require individual skill in preference to more gregarious team-games. In this respect he is different from his father, who excelled in team-games when he was younger. At school Charles's preference for individual sports was largely a result of shyness. In his maturity it appears to take a different form. In individual sports Charles is constantly testing his own skills and pitting himself against personal challenges, without having a team to fall back on. In this relentless desire to better his previous achievements he is able to prove to himself and to others that his success comes from his own efforts and not from the support of others. Far from being selfish and single-minded, this attitude is vitally important for a man whose whole life has been geared to a position that will set him apart from, and in many eyes above, other men.

Like everyone else, Charles is conditioned by his upbringing, and he makes no apology for following the traditional field-sports of the aristocracy and landed

OPPOSITE *During an afternoon of polo at Smiths Lawn, Windsor.*

A swim during a short informal visit to Deauville, France.

gentry among whom he was raised. The one interesting and indicative exception to this general rule is the so-called 'sport of kings' – horse-racing. Though Prince Charles attends Royal Ascot and other race-meetings during the year, he admits that he does not share his mother's love of racing, for the simple reason that he has to be merely a spectator. 'I'm one of those people who don't like sitting around and watching someone else doing something. . . . I don't like going to the races to watch horses thundering up and down. . . . I'd rather be riding the horses myself.'

His love of horses was generated at an early age when he learned to ride a docile pony called William before graduating to an equally benign Shetland called Fun. Though he never showed his sister's instinctive flair, he always enjoyed riding during the school holidays, either at Sandringham or at Balmoral, and continued steadily to improve. But while Anne followed the orthodox pattern of gymkhanas and show-jumping, Charles set his eyes on a different equestrian pastime – polo.

Prince Philip had taken up the game after his marriage in order to share in his bride's enthusiasm for horses. With his customary skill and sporting instinct, he rapidly became a very good player, achieving a handicap of eight at the height of his playing career. The world's top players have a handicap of ten.

Charles had constantly pestered his father to let him play, but Prince Philip felt that his son's mid-teens would be a suitable time for him to make his début in matches. In the meantime, he frequently gave his son lessons on the polo-lawns at Windsor, teaching him the essential skills of pony-handling and ball-control. During matches the young Prince would watch his father from the side, where he helped to prepare the ponies and look after the polo-sticks and refreshments, the job

146

Charles competing recently in a horse race. Like his mother, sister and father, Prince Charles loves horses and horsey sports. Although up to now most of his energies have been concentrated on polo, which he learned from his father, the Prince has recently been widening his interests ...

he would later be delegating to a succession of long-suffering girl-friends.

Bowing to the inevitable, the Princess of Wales nevertheless seems to enjoy attending polo matches, and is an enthusiastic team supporter. Many of the most relaxed pictures of her have been taken at Smith's Lawn, where she is able to be herself among friends with a similar background and interests and also wear the casual, youthful clothes she loves but which are unsuitable for formal appearances. Although an early fall discouraged the Princess from riding she has started to learn again so that she can share more fully in one of her husband's main interests. With the Queen to instruct her the Princess will no doubt regain her confidence, although it is unlikely that she will ever be as enthusiastic as her husband.

'I love the game, I love the ponies, I love the exercise,' is the way Charles once summed up his favourite sport. Polo is obsessive and can easily become a full-time preoccupation. It is also exceedingly expensive. Charles spends in the region of £20,000 a year on the sport, much of which goes on the upkeep and transport of a string of special ponies. Experts point out, however, that this is totally insufficient for the quality of the game he is now playing. His coach even asserts that he has greater natural ability than Prince Philip. Charles, he states, 'is fearless, has great potential strength and a technique that is almost faultless'. He is clearly one of the leading players in the country and is prevented from quickly joining the ranks of the world's top players only by his attitude to his ponies. Apparently he is too gentle with them and never treats them as roughly as the competition of top-class games demands. He also refused to spend the amount of money necessary to maintain a large enough string of top ponies. The calibre of game in which Charles plays demands frequent changes of ponies, which have to be in first-class condition. However, with a good pony costing over £3,000 before you start to keep and feed it,

147

... *He now has a new passion –
cross-country riding, in which
teams of four compete against each
other. Even more recently he has
begun to ride as a jockey in point to
point events, although with mixed
success.*

149

the expense is astronomical by any standards. Charles is obviously conscious of the uproar there would be in some quarters if he spent as much money on polo as his supporters would like him to, though he admits that it is his one real extravagance in life. 'But,' he once remarked, 'if I knew that there was immense criticism of my playing polo, I'd have to think about it. You can't have everything you want, even if you feel it does no harm. People's susceptibilities count.'

However, his enthusiasm is such that he finds games anywhere in the world and at any time of the day. While visiting Ghana, he played one game at 7.30 in the morning in order to fit it in before the temperature soared to one hundred degrees Fahrenheit. The following year he had an opportunity to play some of the world's best players when he was touring South America. He has played in India, where the game was first played by the British, and now plays regularly in France.

At home he tries to play twice a week during the season. The polo dates he can make are entered into his calendar the previous winter, and woe betide any member of his staff who double-books an engagement on any of those days.

His horsemanship is also practised in less-publicized manner on the hunting-field. Although he has been interested in hunting for a long time, Charles has started actually riding to hounds only in recent years. The meets he attends are well-kept secrets, and he usually joins the rest of the field after they have 'moved off', to avoid any adverse publicity. For here again he is sensitive to public opinion and has openly admitted that he would give up hunting if he ever felt that the majority of the public were against his participation.

Charles's skill on horseback is well matched by his expertise with a shotgun. Both he and Prince Philip, who taught him, are rated among the best shots in the country, though some shooting companions claim Prince Charles has now outstripped his father. Their expertise is of course entirely appropriate, since both royal marksmen have access to some of the best shooting in Great Britain. Sandringham provides superb pheasant and partridge shooting, while the moors around Balmoral offer equally good opportunities for grouse. As a bachelor Prince Charles made full use of the opportunities his royal status gives him to enjoy the sport.

It seems, however, that Prince Charles is already slowly being influenced by the opinion of the Princess of Wales, and there has been a marked lessening of his interest in 'bloodsports'. If this is true it will no doubt be welcomed by the RSPCA who once labelled the Prince 'Hooligan of the Year'. The Princess, despite coming from a huntin', shootin' and fishin' aristocratic family, has never relished any form of hunting. She was appalled by the publicity surrounding her one experience of deer stalking and has since followed her own instinct to avoid all sports involving killing. It is a mark of Charles's devotion to his wife that during the 1983/4 season he did not kill a single deer and was notable for his absence from all royal shooting parties: that is a very significant concession by one who has so eloquently defended country sports in the past. As his growing family becomes of paramount interest he may eventually give up shooting, and even hunting, altogether.

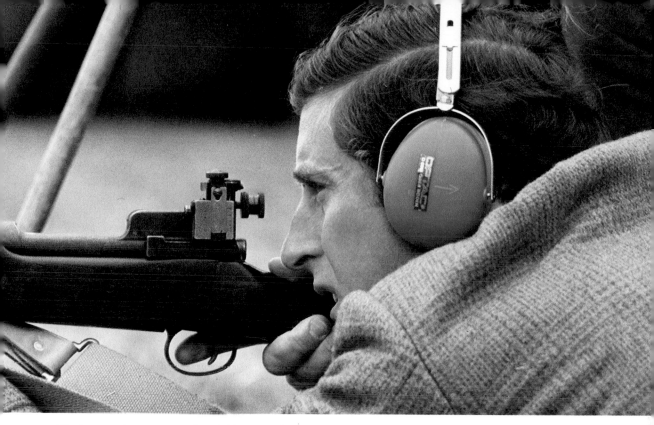

The Prince demonstrates his skills as a rifle shot.

In some respects he has been able to find the danger and excitement of the hunting-field in the thrill of cross-country riding, in which teams of four horsemen attempt to ride from one point to the other in the shortest possible time. In a sense it is like hunting without the fox and hounds. Since taking up the sport in the spring of 1978, Charles has had a fair number of falls, as the fences are often extremely difficult, but in typically good-humoured manner his response has been that it is 'good practice for parachute jumping'. He now runs two teams of his own, the Duke of Cornwall's Chasers and the Earl of Chester's Chasers.

The last of the three traditional sports of the country gentleman's trio, after hunting and shooting, is fishing. Once again the Prince owes his enthusiasm to his father. Nowadays though, it is his grandmother who accompanies him more often than not. They share the quiet, contemplative spirit that is best suited to solitary hours spent by rushing Highland rivers, casting flies to the cautious salmon. Charles is now regarded as the foremost fisherman in the family, even exceeding the Queen Mother's prowess. He has won the unqualified respect of the gillies on the River Dee at Balmoral for his superlative skill. On one occasion during the summer of 1976, when the river was very low and there was no likelihood of any fish being caught, Charles hooked seven salmon in one day – to the astonishment of the experts, one of whom commented afterwards: 'That was a grand effort. I and one or two other gillies had fished solidly for the previous two or three days without taking one fish. Then along comes the Prince of Wales and immediately shows all of us how it should be done.'

Fishing, like polo and shooting, has become a regular fixture in Charles's annual calendar, and before his marriage he often used to spend a week fishing with Lord and Lady Tryon at their lodge in a remote part of Iceland, where the sport is reputed to be as good as anywhere in the world.

There is one sport, however, to which Prince Philip introduced his son, that Charles rather surprisingly does not enjoy a great deal, and that is sailing. Although he crewed for his father on one or two occasions, it became clear that there was frequently some disagreement between them when confined to the limited area of a racing-yacht. Recalling the atmosphere, Charles described it as follows:

I remember one disastrous day when we were racing and my father was, as usual, shouting. We wound the winch harder, and the sail split in half with a sickening crack. Father was not pleased. Not long after, I was banned from the boat after an incident cruising off Scotland. There was no wind, and I was amusing myself taking pot-shots at beer-cans floating around the boat. The only gust of the day blew the jib in front of my rifle just as I fired. I wasn't invited back on board.

He does make certain exceptions to this general dislike, and interestingly the one type of 'sailing' that he has been photographed practising most frequently is the difficult solo sport of wind-surfing. In fact the crew of HMS *Bronington* was frequently amused by the sight of their skipper, clad in a wet-suit, popping over the side to go for a short spin whenever the opportunity arose.

On the whole though, Charles prefers to be in the water rather than skimming over its surface. As a swimmer almost from the age that he could walk, he has revelled in swimming all over the world. From the North Pole to the Pacific and from the Caribbean to the English Channel, he has shown his love of the sea and his interest in marine life. When he first visited Australia, one of the big disappointments was being unable to try his hand at surfing the mighty breakers, which were reckoned too dangerous for a novice while he was there. He has since made up for this, putting the surf-riding skills he learned at Gordonstoun to the test against some of the most powerful waves in the world.

His passion for diving has led him to explore the sea-bed in such exotic surroundings as Fiji and the Caribbean. Waxing lyrical in a diving magazine, he once described the sensation of exploring a wreck off the British Virgin Islands as 'experiencing the extraordinary sensation of swimming inside the hull of an old schooner as if it were some vast green cathedral filled with shoals of fish'.

Charles first appeared on the European ski-slopes while he was at Gordonstoun, but the attentions of the Continental Press prevented his really enjoying himself. Apart from one or two forays to the Scottish slopes and the odd day in Europe, he did not take up the sport again seriously until the beginning of 1978. Then, in the company of the Duke and Duchess of Gloucester and a party of friends, he spent ten days at the Swiss resort of Klosters, and has now become an enthusiast.

The Princess of Wales genuinely shares her husband's love of skiing and is

Prince Charles on a skiing holiday at Klosters. Skiing has become one of his favourite pastimes. The Princess of Wales is also a keen skier.

constantly improving. In January 1983 the couple stayed with the royal family of Lichtenstein for a private skiing holiday which was largely spoilt by the intrusive demands of photographers. In the following year a special photo session was arranged for the world's press after which the Prince and Princess were able to enjoy their skiing holiday in private.

Charles's attitude to skiing, like his attitude to other sports, was well summed up by his great-uncle and close friend for many years, Earl Mountbatten, who said of him, 'He is more fearless than anyone I have met, and he does it because he enjoys trying things out for himself.'

Sport is more than a relaxation for Prince Charles. It is more than a way of escaping from the strictures imposed on him by protocol. It is one of the few ways in which he can compete with other people on more or less equal terms.

As much of his everyday life is so removed from the realm of most people's normal experience, the sight of the mud-spattered Prince of Wales competing in a cross-country event or patiently fishing in the rain is a reassuring indication that the Royal Family are not rarified public objects that seldom stray far from the comfortable security of royal luxury. Sport is also one of the few fields of activity in which excellence can be objectively measured. Few of us can really comprehend the skill involved in flying a helicopter or a jet fighter, but many more who have played some ball-game can appreciate the difficulty of controlling a polo-pony and hitting a ball with a long stick at the same time.

British history may or may not have been determined on the playing-fields of Eton as some historians have fondly believed, but we may be sure that an important chapter of events in the life of Prince Charles was drafted in the rugged surroundings of Gordonstoun.

9

The Private Prince

Whenever Prince Charles is photographed or filmed, he is almost invariably surrounded by people. This is more true than ever now that he is married: the Princess's beauty and style have ensured that the royal couple are two of the most famous people in the world. However, this is the public image of a family whose private life is almost the exact opposite.

Whereas their public life is documented, photographed, praised and criticized in almost every public form, the details of their private life are as closely guarded as the Crown Jewels. As with other members of the royal family the press speculates furiously and endlessly (for example over Prince Charles's girlfriends in his bachelor days), but nothing is really known about how or with whom they spend their 'off-duty' time. This close secrecy is made possible primarily because the Prince has only a very small circle of people he would call close friends. The members of this small band have become intimate friends because Charles is totally able to rely on them not to disclose any confidences he may impart. Indeed, many of them make no outward show of their friendship with him at all, for that very reason.

We all tend to make friends with people with whom we share similar interests and occupations. But if your interests are of the individualist, solo variety and your occupation is to be a future King of Great Britain, then the field of likely 'buddies' is severely restricted.

It is significant that Charles has few associates from his school days who still number among his close friends. The only exception is his cousin Norton Knatchbull, the film-director grandson of Earl Mountbatten, who befriended Charles at Gordonstoun. Apart from him there are few old boys from Cheam or Gordonstoun who call regularly at Buckingham Palace.

Not unnaturally, most of his best friends share Charles's interest in at least one of his favourite pastimes. He met French art expert Guy Wildenstein through playing polo and shares a love of skiing with Charles Palmer-Tomkinson and his wife Patti. However, since his marriage Charles has gradually grown apart from former close friends such as Lord and Lady Tryon, Lord and Lady Tollemache, and the Parker-Bowles who are close neighbours in Gloucestershire. Of course the Princess has

OPPOSITE *Sporting activities give Charles a rare opportunity to be himself and compete on equal terms with others. He is photographed here during a Cotswold Hunt team event.*

introduced him into her own circle of friends, many of whom, although younger, share his love of sport.

There are doubtless others with whom the Prince can indulge his less public interests in history, anthropology, music and drama, about whom the world at large knows very little. But one close friend has been reported as saying that Charles 'most likely doesn't know more than three or four people who you could really describe as intimate pals'.

This is due partly to Charles's position and partly to his introspective nature. When most of your life is spent under constant surveillance, it must be very tempting to want to spend time alone with your family when the opportunity arises. If your life is one of endless introductions, polite small-talk and formal speeches, there can be few things nicer than settling down in the evening to watch a favourite television programme. In Charles's case the favourites are comedy programmes with the brand of zany humour that he and Princess Diana both enjoy, such as *Monty Python's Flying Circus* and *Fawlty Towers*.

One of the many differences between the current Prince of Wales and his two immediate predecessors in the title is that, unlike them, he does not set out to be the leader of a glittering social set. The gambling coterie of Edward VII and the night-club clique of Edward VIII are both anathema to the present Prince of Wales. He dislikes nightclubs and discothèques with their ear-shattering music and smoke-filled atmosphere. Instead he prefers to spend an evening at the theatre or the opera followed by a quiet, intimate dinner.

This does not mean that he avoids parties or shuns the opportunity to have a good time when he is in the mood. The frequent Press photographs of him taking to the floor with scantily clad maidens across the world from Fiji to Rio have shown his skill in and obvious enjoyment of dancing. When he was serving in the Navy, there were times when he and his brother-officers indulged in boisterous final flings ashore, before setting off to sea once again. On one occasion Lieutenant the Prince of Wales was one of a party who stayed revelling in a Caracas nightclub until four o'clock in the morning, with, in the Prince's words, 'a party of beautiful Venezuelan ladies'. However, he recalled that, 'When the ship sailed at 6.30 that morning, I was not in good shape at all.'

But even on occasions like that, there may well have been a subconscious sense of duty that motivated his action. If you have been conditioned to being on display since childhood, switching into the right part must be second nature by the time you reach your mid-twenties.

His upbringing has no doubt contributed to his attitude to older people. While he has lost touch with many of his own contemporaries from school and university, Charles still keeps in touch with many of his older friends. 'I've been brought up with older people, and I've enjoyed it. On the whole, in my youth, I preferred to be with older people,' was the observation of the man who as a child shared the companionship of detectives and chauffeurs when he played football in the park and

Prince Charles, accompanied as ever by his bodyguard, inspects the course before competing in a cross-country event at Cirencester.

who spent two school holidays with a headmaster twenty years his senior.

For all the restrictions on his life, and the factors that limit his activities and easy access to people that the rest of us enjoy, he does not seem to be in the slightest way bitter or resentful, for the lack of close friends and relative lack of freedom are more than compensated for by the happiness Charles finds in his family. 'I've never wanted not to have a home life,' he once confided. 'We happen to be a very close-knit family. I'm happier at home with the family than anywhere else, so I don't feel in any sense that I'm not free.'

There is little doubt that Charles tended to hero-worship his father in his youth. Prince Philip's sporting achievements, his natural ease in company and the respect he commanded from all who met him, made a profound impression on his young son, who was at first the direct opposite of his extrovert father. It was only when Charles's self-confidence began to master his introspective nature that he started to move out of his father's shadow. He shares with Prince Philip a delight in absurd comedy, a taste for adventure and a restless searching after knowledge. But while the father directs his attentions to technology and science, his son still shows an obvious passion for the arts, and history in particular.

In spite of the fact that the first thirty years of his life bore a strong similarity to his father's – with the exception of the time he spent at Trinity College – Charles is adamant that he was never pressurized into following in his father's footsteps. 'His attitude was very simple,' he explained. 'He told me what were the pros and cons of all the possibilities and what he thought was best. Then he left me to decide. I freely subjected myself to what he thought best because I saw how wise he was. By the time

20 November 1979. The Queen and Prince Philip with their family, including Peter Phillips. A picture issued to commemorate their thirty-second wedding anniversary.

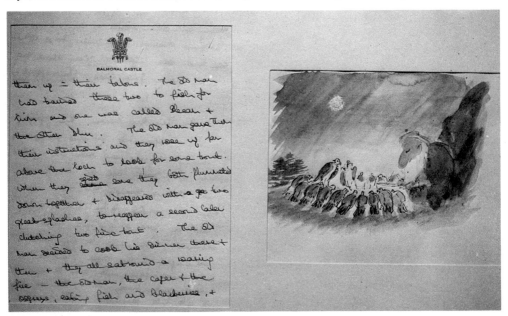

Pages from a story written and illustrated by Prince Charles for his two younger brothers. This has since been published as a best-selling children's book, The Old Man of Lochnagar.

I had to be educated, I had perfect confidence in my father's judgement.'

Although it is now clear that Charles's personality is more like that of his mother, he still shows some signs of emulating his father. They share the characteristic mannerisms of walking with their hands clasped behind their backs and tossing back their heads when they laugh, though Charles no longer displays the rather haughty attitudes he copied from his father when he was still in his teens and less sure of himself.

Many people, not least the Queen Mother, have seen similarities between the Prince and his grandfather, George VI. George VI's diffidence and conscientious attention to duty have been transferred to his grandson through his daughter. Like the Queen, Charles is kind and gentle by nature. Though he has grown more accustomed to public life than she will ever become, he is still happiest trudging over ploughed fields in wellingtons and casting for salmon on the banks of the River Dee.

If Charles takes after his mother, his sister is undeniably her father's daughter. Yet despite the difference in their personalities, Charles and Anne have developed a very close relationship. It is only in the last few years that Princess Anne's relationship with the press has mellowed. When she was younger she seemed unable to submit gracefully to the inevitable demands made on her as a public person, and this was particularly true when she was competing as a private individual at horse shows: the attention of photographers put her at a disadvantage which Prince Charles, having ridden competitively himself, understood perfectly. He once tried to explain her unfortunate outburst directed against reporters and photographers by emphasizing that, while riding competitively, she was under as much stress as any other sporting personality of international status:

> From my sister's point of view the behaviour of the photographers is very hard to take, and I can understand why.
> If you are doing something competitive in public, especially in the top international class, you are inevitably keyed up. To have a lot of people with cameras pursuing you, and possibly frightening the horse, is annoying, to say the least. It is easy to become irritable and to feel that it is only when things go wrong ... that photographs appear in the paper.

He showed equal concern in 1974 when a kidnap-attempt was made on the Princess and her husband Captain Mark Phillips in the Mall. Charles was serving in the Caribbean at the time but was all set to fly straight home to help comfort his sister, until she reassured him that she was really all right and wanted him to stay where he was. Since Princess Anne is married now, with a home of her own, Charles sees less of her than he used to. However, before he bought Highgrove, which is just down the road from Gatcombe Park, he frequently arranged to stay with the Princess and Captain Phillips on his way to official functions in Wales. When they presented him with a nephew, Peter, Charles, who is inordinately fond of babies, had even more reason to call on them whenever the opportunity arose.

His relationship with his younger brothers, Andrew and Edward, is equally close, though now that Prince Andrew is a fully grown man, somewhat taller than Charles and dashingly good-looking, his elder brother cannot exert quite the same watchful authority as he used to. The two brothers are very good friends, they have taken parachuting courses together, and Prince Andrew, in following his brother into the Services, will have as much to live up to as Prince Charles did when he followed his father's footsteps. Prince Edward will soon be as tall as his eldest brother and will be finding his own feet in the public world, following the rest of his family. However, Prince Charles will always be on hand to help and guide him in the future.

At the other end of the spectrum is the Queen Mother, who has always had a special affection for her eldest grandchild, whom she once called 'my gentle little boy'. It is natural that she should be attached to Charles, who so closely resembles the husband to whom she was so deeply attached.

For his own part Charles has always been devoted to his grandmother. She was always a source of comfort during the testing loneliness that he experienced at school, and even now that he has grown into a confident, self-assured man he still corresponds regularly with her while he is away, and Clarence House is always one of the first places he visits when he returns from any of his visits abroad.

He paid her as handsome a tribute as any proud grandmother could wish for, on her birthday in 1978. Writing in a book about the Queen Mother published on her birthday, Charles said:

Ever since I can remember, my grandmother has been the most wonderful example of fun, laughter, warmth, infinite security and, above all else, exquisite taste in so many things.

For me she will always be one of those extraordinary, rare people whose touch can turn everything to gold – whether it be putting people at their ease, turning something dull into something amusing, bringing happiness and comfort to people, or making any house she lives in a unique haven to cosiness and character.

Charles's great-uncle Earl Mountbatten was another member of the older generation whom Charles greatly admired. As the elder statesman of the royal family, Earl Mountbatten played a formative rôle in the lives of both Prince Philip and Prince Charles. He always showed a touching interest in his great-nephew's career, particularly during his time in the Royal Navy. The admiration was mutual, and Charles was always eager to be guided and advised by 'Uncle Dickie's' wisdom and experience.

However, Charles was more than a mere 'yes-man' to his great-uncle's ideas on how he should behave and what stance he should take on certain issues. The Earl once recalled an example of Charles's own brand of determined obstinacy:

I had asked him to speak at the Gandhi Centenary Celebrations, and since I considered I probably knew rather more than he did, I wrote a speech for him. He read it through and then said, 'Would you mind terribly if I didn't use this? I'll write my own and then show it to you for your comments.'

ABOVE *Prince Charles enjoyed a close relationship with his great-uncle Lord Mountbatten. The two are seen here on a visit to Reims in France.* LEFT *The Prince with the rest of his family at the funeral of Lord Mountbatten at Westminster Abbey.*

Well, I looked at what he had written, and I wrote down a list of twelve points. He read them through and then said, 'Would you mind terribly if I don't use these either?'

It was with Lord Mountbatten that Charles first visited India in 1975 on the way to the Coronation of King Birendra in Nepal. While they were in Delhi for a brief stop-over in 1975, Mountbatten took great delight in showing his great-nephew around the Indian capital. He showed him the rooms in the Rashtrapati Bhavan, where he had lived as the last Viceroy of India and for a short time as its first Governor-General.

On Charles's first full-length tour of the sub-continent Earl Mountbatten would have been a source of invaluable information about the country he helped towards liberation in 1947. However, destiny had chosen otherwise, and Charles's great-uncle had been murdered by a terrorist bomb in Ireland the previous August. The shock and horror felt by the Royal Family at that callous act of brutality was written across their faces at the funeral. On his wreath Charles had attached a card eloquently expressing his own deep sense of loss: 'To my HGF and GU from loving and devoted HGS and GN,' it read in their own intimate shorthand. Those who studied it soon deciphered its simple, heartfelt message of farewell: 'To my honorary grandfather and great-uncle from his loving and devoted honorary grandson and great-nephew.'

Now that Charles and Anne are married with children and Andrew and Edward are leading independent lives the traditional Christmas and summer gatherings are firmly written into the royal calendar, and provide valued opportunities for the whole family to be together.

Christmas is traditionally spent at Windsor, where the Royal Family and their staff celebrate the festive season together. After Christmas they move to Sandringham to enjoy the winter countryside of East Anglia. There are shooting-parties and riding, as well as long afternoon walks followed by cosy evenings spent in front of roaring log-fires.

Of all his childhood homes though, Prince Charles's favourite is Balmoral, where the summer holidays are spent. There the family is freer than at any other time of the year. Living the life of Scottish lairds, they can shoot grouse, fish for salmon and meet friends informally on the estate. There are regular events associated with Balmoral that they take a great delight in attending each year. The Highland Games at Braemar are always on the summer calendar of royal visits, so too is the Sunday morning service at the little Crathie kirk near the Castle.

Prince Charles has sometimes been accused of being old-fashioned and conservative in his behaviour and attitudes, but, as he has said himself, that is nothing to be ashamed of. 'If being old-fashioned means fostering a good family atmosphere, then I am proud to be old-fashioned and will certainly remain so.'

Until his early thirties Prince Charles was based at Buckingham Palace. He never felt at home at Chevening, which was for a short time his official residence, and his self-contained apartment in the Palace was comfortable, private and convenient and not oppressively close to his parents. Now he is married Prince Charles, like Princess Margaret and the Gloucesters, has a private apartment in Kensington Palace. However he probably regards Highgrove House in Gloucestershire as his real home. It is a perfect English country house and an ideal base in which to bring up a family.

While the Princess is a leader of fashion the Prince remains conservative in his dress style. His well-groomed, clean-cut appearance is clearly at odds with current trends in which informality and casualness seem to be the orders of the day. He realizes, however, that one of his most important rôles is to set an example to his future subjects. In order to do that, it is important that he behaves naturally and unaffectedly. There must be no hint of contrivance in his manner, since that would immediately suggest an insincerity and artificiality that would damage his image.

Apart from the great range of uniforms that he has to wear, which conform to orthodox military designs, the Prince's clothes are set in a distinctly 'sober' mould. As his tailor once remarked,

The secret is that Prince Charles does not bother about fashion as such. We make his three or four suits a year, and he likes to dress in the classic style we have been making our suits for the past thirty years. He has a nice figure, he is handsome and dresses in a way that befits the first man of the land. He tells me exactly what he wants, and his only real stipulation is that nothing should be too way out.

'Way out' is about the last thing that could be said about the Prince's two-piece, two-buttoned suits, and sadly the fashion-conscious Princess has had little noticeable influence on her husband's wardrobe. In answer to the criticism that his clothes are invariably baggy, Charles explains that, as far as he is concerned, the most important thing about clothes is that they should be comfortable.

Highgrove House, Gloucestershire; a perfect estate set in very traditional, rural countryside.

Prince Charles's clothes may never have excited attention but his long reign as the world's most eligible bachelor certainly did. The shy schoolboy who used to scowl at photographers became one of the most envied men in the world. He was frequently seen in the company of attractive women; but he passed the age of thirty, which he himself mentioned as an age at which he might expect to settle down, without having made a choice.

When he finally announced his engagement the decision came almost as a surprise. He may have taken longer than most young men to choose a wife but then, he had perhaps more to consider than anyone else. When he was only twenty he made it clear that he was well aware that his choice could not be for himself alone.

This is awfully difficult because you have to remember that, when you marry in my position, you are going to marry someone who perhaps one day is going to be Queen. I've got to choose someone very carefully I think who could fill this particular rôle, and it has got to be someone pretty special. I often feel I would like to marry somebody English or perhaps Welsh. Well British anyway.

The matter was further complicated for him by legislation, all of which is centuries old but which still severely restricts the field of choice of a prospective twenty-first-century monarch.

Until the Prince was twenty-five years old, the Queen held a veto over his choice of bride, under the Royal Marriage Act of 1772. By that Act, any descendant of King George II (other than the offspring of British Princesses who married into foreign royal families) must obtain permission from the Crown to marry. Over the age of twenty-five, British Princes and Princesses must still seek the monarch's consent, but, if that is withheld, they may marry without royal permission after giving a year's notice to the Privy Council.

Though Prince Charles was well beyond the age of needing his mother's official approval to his marriage, he was still bound by the legal provision of 1689 which prohibits the marriage of anyone in the royal line of succession with a member of the Catholic Church. (For that reason Prince Michael of Kent renounced his place in the royal succession at the time of his marriage.) Nor, since the Church of England refuses to sanction the re-marriage of divorcés by church rite, could a Prince of Wales, future Head of the Anglican Church, contemplate marriage with a divorcée. That was the reason for his great uncle Edward VIII's abdication in 1936.

So, Prince Charles could only have married a Catholic or a divorcée if he had renounced his claim to the throne. And if the Queen had chosen to withhold her consent for any other reason it would have been extremely embarrassing. It never seemed likely that the Prince would consider any action that might have meant rocking the boat in the way that Edward VIII's abdication had done. Nonetheless as he grew older the possibilities seemed to narrow down alarmingly as suitable girls of around his own age married. Only two European Princesses were seriously considered, and both were Catholics. Princess Caroline of Monaco and the Prince quite clearly never had anything in common and she has married, divorced and re-

Princess Maria-Astrid of Luxembourg (left) *and Lady Jane Wellesley* (right) – *two likely candidates for the position of Princess of Wales before Prince Charles met Lady Diana.*

married since her meeting with Prince Charles in 1977. Princess Marie-Astrid of Luxembourg seemed eminently more suitable as a future Queen, it was rumoured that our own Queen liked her a lot, but her religion was against her. Moreover Prince Charles himself was clearly not attracted to her. The eventual denial from Buckingham Palace which put paid to any further rumours of a possible marriage was as forthright as it is possible to be.

They are not getting married this Monday, next Monday, the Monday after, or any other Monday, Tuesday, Wednesday or Thursday. They do not know each other, and people who do not know each other do not get engaged. The Royal Family do not go in for arranged marriages. If the Prince and Princess Marie-Astrid have met at all, then it has been briefly at official functions.

The Princess herself has since married a German count.

Among the other temporary favourites who made an appearance over the years are Lady Davina Sheffield, whose previous boyfriend revealed that they had lived together; beautiful Sabrina Guinness of the brewery family; Amanda Knatchbull, the grand-daughter of Lord Mountbatten; Anna Wallace with whom he had a much publicized quarrel during a ball at Windsor Castle; and Lady Jane Wellesley.

Lady Jane was considered a serious possibility for a long time and understandably so. She is beautiful, intelligent, and, as a daughter of the Duke of Wellington, she comes from the type of family with which Charles has a great deal in common, and which gives a good grounding in the social graces likely to be needed by a future Queen. The pressure which public speculation put on the romance,

LEFT *Lady Diana manages to remain amused by the hordes of journalists who dogged her relentlessly before her engagement was announced.*

OPPOSITE *The by now 'classic' picture of Lady Diana with two of her charges when she was tricked by a photographer into standing against the light.*

together with Charles's long absences with the Navy, eventually brought it to a close, although the two remain friends. Not surprisingly, one of Charles's subsequent romances was with a girl from a similar background, Lady Sarah Spencer, eldest daughter of Earl Spencer. In February 1978 she halted marriage speculation by saying very firmly, 'I would not marry a man I did not love, whether it was a dustman or the King of England. If he asked me I would turn him down.'

Such an indiscreet denial immediately put paid to the rumours, and, for a short time, to the friendship between the Prince and Lady Sarah. However the Spencer family has too many connections with the Royal Family, going back over centuries, for the rift to last. It did however, attract all the attention to one daughter of the family and for a while the Press and the public forgot that Lady Sarah had sisters, in particular one sister who had always seemed the baby but who in fact was rapidly growing into a most attractive young woman.

The four Spencer children, Sarah, Jane, Diana and their brother, Viscount Althorp, grew up at Park House, on the Sandringham estate. This was their father's home until 1975 when he inherited the title of Earl Spencer, and with it Althorp Hall, a stately home in Northamptonshire. The Spencer children were perfectly at home at Sandringham and Lady Diana was great friends with Prince Andrew and Prince Edward, who are both much nearer her age than Prince Charles.

Prince Charles first really noticed Lady Diana as a potential wife rather than a playmate of his brothers' in the summer of 1980, about the time of her nineteenth birthday, although during the interview given at the time of their engagement he remembered being aware of her as a jolly sixteen-year-old. By the middle of

Prince Charles and Lady Diana chat to Princess Grace of Monaco at Goldsmith's Hall. Lady Diana's striking dress allayed fears that she would slip into a staid fashion style as soon as she married into the Royal Family.

September newspapermen had become aware of his interest and were beginning to pursue Lady Diana to and from the Young England nursery school where she worked. Canny newspaper photographers took photographs of her working with the children against the light to reveal her legs through her thin cotton skirt. Understandably Lady Diana was embarrassed by being caught out by the wily press men and said 'I don't want to be remembered for not having a petticoat.'

One of the least attractive aspects of the much-publicized courtship was the constant emphasis being put upon Lady Diana's 'purity', as though she was a parcel of goods and not a human being. Although it is clearly best if the future Queen of England can steer clear of scandal of any kind, it seems unnecessary for her to have to hear people discussing her blameless past. As she herself said in her straightforward way, at nineteen she hadn't had time to have a past!

As the speculation became fiercer and the press attention more unrelenting Lady Diana impressed everyone with her commonsense, dignity and tact. By November, as the Prince was about to celebrate his thirty-second birthday, many people were sure it would be chosen as the date to announce his engagement. Especially since the Queen herself was reported as saying 'She is a delightful girl'.

However, 15 November came and went without any announcement. Prince Charles completed his tour of India on 12 December but Lady Diana was not there to greet him, nor did she join the Royal Family over Christmas. However she did spend some time at Sandringham in January and speculation started up all over again, despite the fact that Prince Charles did not take her to Klosters for his skiing holiday.

168

At last on 23 February Lady Diana went to see the Queen at Buckingham Palace and the engagement was officially announced on 24 February. Charles it seems had finally asked Lady Diana to marry him at the beginning of February, a few days before she flew to Australia for a private holiday with her mother, Mrs Frances Shand-Kydd, and her step-father. Presumably this was to give her time to reflect on her answer, but with charming frankness Lady Diana said during the engagement interview 'I never had any doubts about it.'

Nor can anyone have had any doubts about Lady Diana's suitability for the demanding position of Princess of Wales. Her family background is ideal. The Spencers' connections with the Royal Family are of very long standing. Diana's father, the eighth Earl Spencer, was once equerry to the Queen. Her grandmother, Lady Fermoy, is an old friend of the Queen Mother and her senior Lady-in-Waiting. Royal protocol and formality are therefore quite familiar to the new Princess.

As for being a useful ambassadress and representative for Britain it would be hard to think that Prince Charles could have chosen anyone more suitable. Diana, in spite of her friends' nickname, 'shy Di', is a self-possessed and charming young woman who clearly makes friends everywhere she goes. In spite of her youth she has great composure, and on a more superficial level she is extremely attractive to look at; everyone loves a Princess but a beautiful Princess is a constant source of interest and delight. Immediately after her engagement Diana showed that she was going to be a wonderful advertisement for the very best of British fashion. The stunning black taffeta off-the-shoulder dress chosen for her first public appearance with Prince Charles created a sensation. It was designed by a young British couple, David and Elizabeth Emanuel. A few days after the black evening dress was admired at Goldsmith's Hall it was announced that the same designers were to design Lady Diana's wedding dress. By choosing the Emanuels Diana made it clear she was not to be overruled by others in her choice of wardrobe, and gave a welcome boost to a new generation of designers.

From the personal point of view the newly engaged couple had a great deal in common. At that moment they were clearly very much in love, 'Whatever in love means' as Prince Charles said on the day their engagement was announced. But, as the Prince clearly knows, it is the friendship which underlies that love which is going to matter just as much later on, especially for two people who will be forced to live so much of their private lives in public. The age difference between the Prince and his wife is the same as the age difference between the Princess's mother and father, who were divorced when Lady Frances was thirty-one. This coincidence must have crossed their minds. When asked about it the Prince replied 'Lots of people have got married with that sort of difference. You are as old as you feel. Diana will help me stay young.'

The inevitable differences resulting from the disparity in age will be more than compensated for by the number of things they have in common: the same type of family background, the same social circle, a great love of serious music as well as the louder modern variety, and a preference for outdoor pursuits (skiing in particular), although Diana is not keen on horse-riding. 'I fell off a horse and lost my nerve,' she says. They also have dislikes in common. Neither cares for noisy nightclubs and the jet-set social scene. Diana preferred not to come out as a débutante and, like the Prince, would rather have a few friends quietly round for a dinner party than go to a rowdy social function. Most important of all they share the same sense of humour and a love of children.

Unlike Queen Mary, who was a reluctant mother, the Princess of Wales has always loved children. When she began her relationship with Prince Charles she was working, like many girls of her age and background, in a private London nursery school. Eventually she might have expected to open her own small school, and perhaps combine running it with having a family of her own. Her early practical experience of children will undoubtedly have helped her in equipping the nursery wing at Highgrove.

Highgrove is a perfect family home. It was bought for about a million pounds from the Macmillan family. The house is Georgian with a colonnaded porch. It has a magnificent entrance hall, a drawing-room, a dining-room, a study, a library and a billiard room. On the first floor there are the principal bedroom suites, four in all, and the nursery wing. On the second floor are five further bedrooms and two bathrooms. The house has been completely refurbished at a cost of £250,000 by designer Dudley Poplack, but the style remains traditionally English and the overall 'feel' of the place has been preserved. Neither the Prince nor the Princess is renowned for their *avant-garde* taste. An additional benefit of the house is that it is one of several royal homes in the Cotswolds. Princess Anne's house, Gatcombe Park, is a mere eight miles away; Prince and Princess Michael of Kent have bought Lypiatt Manor near Stroud; furthermore the Prince's friends, Andrew and Camilla Parker-Bowles, live nearby. So the children of the Prince and Princess of Wales will have plenty of cousins and friends close-at-hand to play with.

Altogether the Prince and Princess of Wales seem to be an ideally suited couple leading what many of us would consider an ideal life. The public aspect of it will undoubtedly prove trying and tiring from time to time, yet the care with which the Prince has chosen his life's partner and their very obvious affection for one another makes it certain that they will overcome the disadvantages of their situation as well as enjoy the great advantages it also brings. Our future Queen has already won the admiration of the public. She will surely show time and time again that the world's most eligible bachelor has at last chosen the world's most perfect wife, for himself and for the country.

OPPOSITE *This serene formal portrait of Lady Diana, taken by Lord Snowdon, appeared in* Vogue *during the height of the pre-engagement press hysteria. It contrasts sharply with the many action shots of her looking slightly harrassed which were appearing in the daily press.*

10

The Future King and Queen

After the excitement of the announcement of their engagement, Charles and Diana did not have long before the wedding which was to turn Lady Diana Spencer into the wife of the Heir to the throne and his future Queen.

I didn't suddenly wake up in my pram one day and say 'Yippee'. I think it just dawns on you slowly that people are interested in you, and you slowly get the idea that you have a certain duty and responsibility. I think it's better that way, rather than someone suddenly telling you.

This was Prince Charles's explanation of his own gradual realization that one day he would inherit his mother's crown. A consciously careful up-bringing had helped him to come to terms with his unique destiny, to appreciate the privileges of his position without losing his sense of perspective. It is patently obvious that the Prince, by nature as well as education, has a strong sense of duty, combined with an acute awareness of the moral and social issues of our century. Many of his speeches emphasize the importance of preserving our environment and of curbing pollution; in his own Duchy of Cornwall he is trying to encourage rural industries and crafts. His good nature is well-known and he makes many personal donations to charity. An example was his sponsorship in the 1984 London Marathon of Bernard Wood, who had approached him privately and without expecting any response: Mr Wood was running to raise money for the Morecambe Bay Clinic, an offshoot of the pioneering Bristol Cancer Clinic which the Prince had opened in 1983. The Prince takes an interest in holistic medicine that is wholly consistent with his general caring approach to the major issues of the day, and his unique position allows him at times to play a truly formative rôle. It is fair to say that his significant speech on the subject to the BMA prompted a more open-minded approach from the practitioners of conventional medicine to the whole issue of the part our minds play in the overall health of our bodies. There is no doubt that the Prince takes very seriously the potential influence his position allows him to exert.

For this earnest approach to the job of Heir Apparent he has to thank the Queen, who has herself enhanced the reputation of the Crown in the twentieth century by

OPPOSITE *Diana gives her first wave as Princess of Wales, as the couple emerge from St Paul's to an overwhelming reception.*

173

The official wedding photographer was Patrick Lichfield, a cousin of the Queen. As well as the families of both the bride and groom, those present included Queen Beatrix of the Netherlands, Princess Grace of Monaco, Princess Gina and Prince Franz of Lichtenstein, Princess Alice and close friends of the couple.

the serious attitude with which she regards her own position. The Queen was only twenty-six when her father died and she ascended the throne. She had lived for sixteen years with the knowledge that she would be Monarch, but despite her father's guidance and her own deep-seated sense of duty, the task that she faced in 1952 must have seemed awesome, even overwhelming, to her at the time.

For that reason, therefore, she resolved to prepare her eldest son right from the start. Throughout his education and slow emergence into public life, his mother was in the background counselling, advising, directing and instructing him with that single goal in mind. Charles was initiated into the mysterious contents of the red despatch-boxes that daily provide the Queen with details of Cabinet meetings and other confidential government business. He was encouraged to meet influential men as he grew older, and he was given the added advantage of mixing with and being advised by experienced statesmen and politicians, such as Earl Mountbatten, Harold Wilson and Rab Butler. As a consequence he has emerged the most carefully trained and well-informed Heir Apparent of recent times.

Diana Spencer has had none of this careful grooming for the rôle which she is now expected to play. Of course the life of consort is not as demanding as that of

During her first months as Princess of Wales, Diana's eagerness to look correct on public occasions led to a style of dress rather too old for her years. . . The glamorous style that is now so recognizable developed as confidence in her own taste grew.

monarch but it has many pitfalls and in some ways being the partner of the person who actually wears the crown can have its own disadvantages.

Whatever the bride's own personal anxieties may have been, the wedding of HRH The Prince of Wales with The Lady Diana Spencer was a triumph for the Royal Family, proving once again that nobody can stage ceremonial events quite as well as the British, and revealing the strength and sincerity of the affection of ordinary people for the Monarchy.

The ninth Princess of Wales gave every indication of future success in the job for which she was not born but for which she is so clearly suited. Of course one of the major elements in her success is her appearance, and on her wedding day she became the perfect fairytale Princess. Her dress was designed by David and Elizabeth Emanuel whose creations so perfectly evoke the storybook charm of being a Princess. They capture a fantasy which the new Princess of Wales has seemed to bring true with evident enjoyment, for it is almost as much of a novelty to her as it is to any little girl whose childhood dream is to marry a Prince and live happily ever after in a palace. The frothy creation which the Emanuels designed for her was made up of forty-four yards of ivory silk produced at Britain's only silk farm at

175

Lullingstone in Dorset. It was encrusted with mother of pearl and thousands of sequins, with a neckline which gave an impression of plunging while at the same time being decorously surrounded by lace frills and a bow which has become one of the hallmarks of the Princess's fashion style. Elaborate precautions had been taken to keep the design a secret, to the extent of cordoning off the street whenever Diana arrived for a fitting. Even on that first day as Princess of Wales her future importance as an ambassadress for British fashion was apparent. For from the minute the press embargo on the design was lifted at 10.35 am, copyists from fashion houses all over the world were poised to reproduce the marvellous dress and get it into the shops by the next day.

The Princess may be less aware of the effect she has on the livelihood of people like the vendors of soft drinks and hamburgers, who did such a roaring trade in the capital that day.

During the ceremony of an hour and ten minutes, the Princess promised to love and honour, but not to obey. A small gesture to modernity maybe but one which Princess Anne had not made eight years earlier and an indication that Diana is a child of her own generation, not prepared to go along with all the traditions of her new family if they do not suit her. This independent approach will have made her very popular with young people, and the Princess has shown in a short time that she can make a unique contribution to the public profile of the Monarchy by keeping its appeal fresh for yet another generation.

Yet another element of the Princess's rôle was revealed by the large number of official guests who helped fill St Paul's Cathedral, among them Nancy Reagan. One of the most useful jobs done by the Royal Family today is to help maintain friendly personal relations with heads of foreign countries. By inviting people to take part in 'family' events like the wedding of her son the Queen is able to reinforce the impression she gives to visiting dignitaries that they are her own personal friends, and thus to strengthen Britain's ties with other nations. Simply by getting married the Princess of Wales was starting to earn her keep.

When she and Prince Charles stood at the top of the Cathedral steps after the wedding Diana's first wave as Princess of Wales was therefore not just a personal acknowledgment of the enthusiasm of the crowds; it was her first engagement in a job to which she had just formally committed herself in front of 750 million people the world over.

It must have been an awesome moment for a young girl without any of the years of training which her husband has had to help him, but it would be wrong to imply that Diana Spencer is a person who came to the position of Princess of Wales without any idea of what lay in store for her. During her interview at the time of the engagement, she declared that she was not afraid of taking on the responsibility, knowing that Prince Charles was there to help her. Coming from her background she had a pretty accurate idea of what her future life would involve. Her family tree goes back to Charles II and James II in the seventeenth century, albeit through their illegitimate children. Her father, Earl Spencer, lives in one of the country's most imposing stately homes, Althorp, surrounded by priceless works of art. When Diana was a young child she and her two sisters and brother lived at Park House on the Sandringham royal estate in Norfolk. The house had originally been made available to her maternal grandfather, Lord Fermoy, who was a friend of George VI. Earl Spencer had married Lord Fermoy's daughter while he himself was equerry to the Queen. Diana is a contemporary of Prince Andrew and Prince Edward and much of her holidays from her fashionable boarding school, West Heath, were spent in their company. The two young Princes were always glad to be able to use the swimming pool at Park House! So Diana Spencer grew up to be on easy terms with the Royal Family and at the same time aware of the tremendous formality and protocol which surround their lives; for even close acquaintances have to be acutely observant of the boundary between friendship and over-familiarity. Earl Spencer, as a former equerry, would also have been 'au fait' with the even more elaborate procedure which is involved on formal occasions.

The Princess of Wales was therefore at a great advantage when it came to absorbing what was required of her in her new rôle. Indeed Prince Charles, however much he may have been attracted to her, must also have been very conscious of this added bonus in her favour.

Prince Charles receives a garland from an elephant in Pipli Village, India.

Charles seized a chance to shake the dust of India's cities off his feet during his 1980 tour and went trekking in the tranquil Pokhara Valley. The distant mountain is Machha Puckhare.

Despite her background, as soon as the engagement was officially announced Diana was spirited away forever from her flat in Coleherne Court and plunged into a crash course of 'Do's and Don'ts' at Buckingham Palace, under the watchful eye of the Queen Mother. By her wedding day she could be relied on to play her part without a hitch. The Queen Mother clearly likes her favourite grandson's wife and must have felt a great sense of fellow feeling towards her, for she too was an Earl's daughter unexpectedly elevated to the rôle of prospective Queen of England. Under her watchful eye Diana learned the rudiments of what would be expected from her, right down to the details of how to achieve that royal wave in the least tiring and most dignified fashion – from the elbow. The friendship which was formed during that brief hothouse period between the engagement and the wedding has clearly lasted and it is obvious that the two are very much at ease in each other's company.

In spite of the sympathetic support of the Queen Mother and the solicitous manner of Prince Charles, those early weeks were clearly a great strain, even for someone whose life had up to then been so close to the Royal Family. One of the hardest things to accept, and one of the aspects of the job which the Princess still finds unbearable at times, is the constant attention of photographers, who will stop at nothing to get the shots they want. Frightening too was the endless series of images of herself with which the future Princess was faced. The press attention made her terribly conscious of the way she looked. Not happy with the charming but rather naive portraits of a nice girl with a bit of puppy fat but good hair and skin, the Princess began a strict dietary regime which made it necessary for the Emanuels to make constant adjustments to the wedding dress right up until the last moment.

Obsession with her weight seemed to dog the Princess again a year later when she fought to regain her figure in record time after the birth of Prince William. Yet while it is easy for journalists, as they did at the time, to draw attention to the Princess's weight loss and to publish photographs showing her looking almost unattractively bony while making dark references to her elder sister Sarah's bout of anorexia nervosa, it is difficult for the Princess to allow herself to relax over her appearance.

One of the main areas in which she at present 'earns her keep' is in the amazing boost she has given to British design and fashion. With the help of a little extra grooming and a more sophisticated hairstyle she has proved almost overnight to have the kind of public appeal formerly exerted only by film stars. Her picture adorns magazines all over the world and in spite of the restrictions imposed on her by the many formal occasions she is required to attend, her clothes reflect a style and fashion consciousness not usually associated with the principle members of the Royal Family.

As confidence in her own judgement and ability to choose designers grows, Diana's clothes get better and better, and correspond closer to the way she wants to look. Immediately after her wedding, when she was still mesmerized by the total immersion in royal know-how which she had recently undergone, Diana's wardrobe showed many of the hallmarks of her older in-laws. In some photographs she looked positively middle-aged, for example at the Ascot week which preceded her wedding. But the Princess is at a great advantage for someone who carries the flag for the best of British fashion: she clearly loves clothes. In 1983 she was reputed to have spent at least £50,000 on clothes, which is not difficult when evening dresses from her favourite designers are priced in thousands of pounds.

While expenditure of this kind may frighten Prince Charles as he balances the books to keep a wife and growing family on the proceeds of the Duchy of Cornwall which once had only to supply his needs, he must also be delighted to see the

LEFT *The Prince and Princess of Wales both enormously enjoy the skiing holiday that has become an established feature of their year. A new policy of an official press call at the start of the holiday ensures that the remainder of their time is truly private.*

RIGHT *Charles and Diana willingly entered into the spirit of things by wearing Edwardian dress during their visit to the 'frontier town' of Fort Edmonton, Canada. Diana seemed rather more at home in her costume than Charles did in his.*

phenomenal success the Princess is enjoying in this particular capacity. Nor can he have been unaware that when the Princess has arrived somewhere in an outfit already given publicity at a previous engagement people have expressed disappointment not to have been complimented by a totally new ensemble. New clothes are not mere self-indulgence for a Princess of Wales.

One area where the Princess has turned the necessity to follow royal tradition into her own stunningly brilliant fashion style has been in the wearing of hats. After one or two unfortunate early ventures, like the blue creation which appeared at the 1981 Trooping the Colour, she has forged for herself a style and an individuality that is original, innovative and exciting. Now she and her milliner, John Boyd, come up with hats which are suitable both to the occasion and to a young person. Probably the most successful shape of all has been the small felt tricorne with elaborate feather trim. She wore one of these with her going-away outfit and it has appeared many times since in various colours and with minor variations. The tricorne has been the most widely copied of all her hats. She has made hats the big fashion news for young people, and is now known to the millinery trade as their patron saint; for it is no exaggeration to say that she has pulled the industry out of the doldrums virtually single-handed.

There is a theatricality in much of the Princess's dress which ensures that she is constantly newsworthy. That fantasy element which is so obvious in her evening gowns is becoming increasingly apparent in her day clothes. Two of her favourite designers, the Belville Sassoon partnership, came up with a Russian Cossack-style coat with bold braid frog-fastening down the front, and a hat trimmed with a bow on the side. The muff which completed the Anna Karenina look was entirely responsible for the short-lived fashion for muffs in the winter of 1981! There was a similar 'snow princess' feel to the luxurious green velvet suit with its full skirt and peplum waist which the Princess wore on her solo trip to Oslo in February 1984.

While other women can hope to emulate Diana's style of dressing with cheaper copies of her clothes, few if any can ever aspire to the fabulous jewellery which she is now privileged to wear. Such jewellery these days is rarely seen on any but the most wealthy of women. Diana was not totally unfamiliar with good jewellery, and wore the Spencer family tiara to hold her wedding veil in place; but until that great day her jewellery was noticeable only for its simplicity. The single adornment thought worthy of notice was the letter 'D' which she wore round her neck on a simple gold chain. Now she wears jewels which are the match of any in the world. She continues to wear the Spencer tiara on many occasions requiring formal evening dress but now has the alternative of the tiara which used to belong to Queen Mary. The Spencer tiara is a fairly simple scroll design entirely suitable for a young woman. Queen Mary's tiara is much more regal and emphasizes the point that the Princess of Wales is a future Queen of England. The tiara was much in evidence on the 1983 tour of Australia, New Zealand and Canada; at the state banquet given at Auckland on the eve of the couple's departure from New Zealand, the Princess wore it with a cream-coloured ball gown designed by Gina Fratini. Such jewels, including the impressive pearl and diamond drop earrings which she often wears with the tiara, do not belong to Diana in the true sense. They are hers to use but not to sell. Like the fabulous collection of jewellery owned by the Queen, Diana's formal jewellery is held in trust for the next generation. This is not true of her magnificent engagement ring, a large sapphire surrounded by diamonds. It was made by Garrard's at a cost of around £40,000. It belongs entirely to the Princess and is the one piece of jewellery which has been extensively copied, although usually for prices only a fraction of the cost of the real thing.

If being a leader of fashion and an encouragement for British fashion exporters has proved a rôle which the Princess of Wales has positively welcomed, so too has being a mother. Primitive as it may sound it is one of the main tasks of any Princess of Wales to produce an Heir to the Heir. Fortunately Diana loves children, as many photographs with them show, so producing her own has been a welcome aspect of her job. Prince William was born less than a year after her marriage. Motherhood takes a lot of adaptability at the best of times and particularly so soon after marriage and taking on a rôle as demanding as that of Princess of Wales; yet Diana has

OPPOSITE *This head-and-shoulders portrait shows in detail the fine Spencer tiara that Diana wore at her wedding. Now a Princess, she is often to be seen wearing the even more fabulous tiara once worn by Queen Mary.*

clearly thrived on maternity. Her approach to her first pregnancy was straight-forward and apart from missing some appearances because of morning sickness she carried on working fairly normally. In this again she showed herself typical of her generation, though it must be said that Princess Anne's matter-of-fact approach to the whole business helped to pave the way. Indeed so much did Diana take it all in her stride that Prince Charles had occasionally to be reprimanded for expecting her to go out with him while he was shooting. Naturally the Princess's maternity clothes were closely watched for fashion detail and as usual she did not disappoint her audience. Her clothes were comfortable while also stylish, with her fondness for detailed necklines proving a useful distraction from the waistline. However, she did not rush into obvious maternity clothes in either of her two pregnancies. A few days after the announcement in February 1984 that she was expecting a second child she was photographed in a stunning white evening tuxedo. While pregnant with Prince William she stayed comfortable in trousers and the colourful hand-knitted jumpers (some of them belonging to Prince Charles) which have become one of the trade-marks of her informal wardrobe.

After the birth of Prince William the Princess, through conscious efforts, slimmed down very quickly and seemed to take on a more mature and sleek elegance than before.

The Prince and Princess of Wales have a subtly different approach to their family than might have been expected from past royal parents. One wonders how many men may have been influenced by the Prince's characteristic belief that fathers should be present at the birth of their children. The Princess, unlike her mother-in-law, produced the future Prince of Wales not at Buckingham Palace but in the delivery room at St Mary's Hospital, Praed Street, Paddington. Like most modern mothers she was up and about very rapidly and took the new Prince home the next day, although mothers whose home life was not quite so smoothly organized for a new mother were warned against rushing to follow suit. Charles set a good example to other fathers by carrying his son himself, as the proud parents emerged from the hospital. He clearly takes a much closer interest in his son than many of his forbears. It would be hard to imagine even Prince Philip carrying his son off a plane in a carrycot, yet Prince Charles obviously relishes being involved with his family.

Although their nanny, Barbara Barnes, is an essential part of the household, it is quite clear that the Prince and Princess of Wales have no intention of allowing the demands on their time to make them remote from their children. It soon became obvious that Prince William was to accompany his parents on their long tour of Australia, New Zealand and Canada when he was almost a year old. It may now seem a happy and satisfactory solution, but for some time there was real doubt that they might be allowed to take him. There were rumours that Diana was threatening not to go if it meant parting from her son and there were few members of the public who did not sympathize with her and like her the more because of it. Perhaps no-one had seriously considered the possibility before; or maybe previous generations of

ABOVE *Despite a difference in their ages of 60 years, the Queen Mother and the Princess of Wales have struck up a firm friendship based on mutual affection and respect.*

RIGHT *Diana's much-publicized love of children is not simply a story got up by the press: it is clearly genuine, and reciprocated by her young audiences.*

the Royal Family had been brainwashed into believing that 'nanny knows best' – and that meant a regular supply of marmite sandwiches (no foreign food) and being tucked up in your own bed every night even if there were no mother there to kiss you good night. It is probable that the Queen remembered her own sadness at being parted from the young Prince Charles and Princess Anne for nearly six months during her post-Coronation tour of the Commonwealth in 1953/4. She eventually gave the necessary consent for two Heirs to the throne and a future Queen of England to travel together in the same aeroplane, and the tour went ahead as a family affair.

The tour of Australia, New Zealand and Canada lasted from mid-March to the beginning of July 1983, and was a turning-point in many ways for the Prince and Princess of Wales. Maybe because she had William with her the Princess felt able to relax and enjoy the experience, but everyone noted a new confidence in her which increased daily as she and the people of the three different countries responded warmly to each other. Probably she felt more relaxed on this, her first overseas tour, precisely because it *was* overseas and she felt less closely scrutinized by the rest of the family. Whatever the reason, in retrospect it is seen as the first time the Princess showed her full potential as a member of the royal team. It was also fascinating to see that Prince Charles himself was having to learn a new rôle he may not have been prepared for at the time of his marriage, that of playing second fiddle to his wife. Indeed as the crowds called out 'We want Diana' he was heard to remark ruefully that he could really do with two wives. The tour illustrated very well one of the most important functions of the future King and Queen: to represent the Monarch and help take some of the burden off her shoulders by making people in all corners of the Commonwealth feel that they get their fair share of royal attention. In Australia and Canada, however, the Prince and Princess of Wales were able to achieve something which even the Queen cannot. Although the Queen's own tour of Australia in September 1981 was a huge success there was no doubt that a substantial number of people, while admiring the Queen personally, felt that Australia should really be a Republic. In Canada, with its French Canadian citizens, there has long been a vociferous minority calling for a Republic. As the Queen gets older and seems more remote to many of the younger people in those countries, her position as monarch becomes less comprehensible to them. Each new generation seems further away from the country of origin of the first settlers. Charles and Diana at least seem closer in age and interests. The extreme youth of the Princess of Wales has been a big

OPPOSITE ABOVE *Relaxed occasions like polo matches give Diana the opportunity to leave her formal clothes in the wardrobe and appear in the stylish, casual outfits she personally prefers.*

OPPOSITE BELOW *Typical of her generation, Princess Diana shunned unflattering maternity clothes for as long as possible, and improvised with clothes she already owned – and some, like this sweater, owned by Prince Charles!*

bonus to the Monarchy in 'capturing' that particular market. A Princess who listens to the latest groups on her personal headphone set, who buys casual clothes from the same chain stores as many of her contemporaries, who is not too decorous to give her husband a big kiss as soon as she sees the photographers have put their cameras down, is bound to make the Monarchy seem pertinent and accessible to young people, as it seemed to their parents. Indeed that may be why the Princess so visibly blossomed on this long tour, for at last she could see the purpose of the job she was doing. Although she admitted to Newfoundland Premier Brian Peckford that she found her position as Princess of Wales a strain she felt able to add 'I feel I am doing my job better now than I was before.'

Back home the country where she may get the same sense of accomplishment is Wales, which also has its fair share of people anxious to change the status quo and to obtain a longed-for independence. The first major engagement which the Prince and Princess of Wales took on after their honeymoon and summer family holiday at Balmoral was a three-day tour of their Principality in October 1981. In that time they visited eighteen towns. The Princess illustrated her burgeoning fashion flair by wearing an off-the-peg suit in the colours of the Welsh flag – red and green. She also showed willing, if not much skill, in attempting a few words of Welsh and was photographed (an indication of things to come) with large numbers of children. Fortunately Diana has not allowed her 'training' to interfere too much with the spontaneity which makes people warm to her. Whereas other members of the Royal Family incline from the waist to receive a bouquet from a small child, the Princess squats right down so that she can chat face to face. Nor is she averse to being touched by the children who inevitably want to pat her. Even when she faces a heavy schedule of hand shaking she prefers not to wear gloves. As well as her obvious rapport with children she has a sympathetic approach to the old and is happy to bring herself down to a face-to-face level with those who are too frail to stand. Combined with this relaxed approach is an informal line of chat which leaves those introduced to her with a delightful feeling of having taken part in a real conversation, not just polite small talk. While expecting her second child the Princess confided to women at a Leicester knitwear factory that she had not felt well since the outset, adding 'I'm not made for the production line, but it is all worthwhile in the end.'

For the Princess one of the disadvantages of pregnancy is that she cannot accompany her husband on all his trips, and in March 1984 the Prince of Wales was reluctantly forced to make his month-long tour of Tanzania, Zambia, Zimbabwe and Botswana alone. Although clearly the health risks to the Princess would have been too great, he must have hated to leave her at that time. The Prince would have been especially anxious to show Zimbabwe to the Princess, for he represented the Queen at its formal transfer to black government in 1980. Knowing how much she had enjoyed the sight-seeing aspect of the tour of Australia, New Zealand and Canada he will have missed showing Diana the Great Zimbabwe complex – the

Prince Charles demonstrates his intention of participating fully in all aspects of being a parent, including holding the baby.

remains of an ancient royal residence from which the country takes its new name. The stone buildings go back to what is known as the middle ages in Europe. For the Prince, who read archaeology and anthropology at Cambridge and who remains keenly interested in all aspects of history, the chance to see such sites is one of the big compensations for a life which is largely organized to suit other people.

They do not always have a choice when planning their schedule, but the Prince and Princess can exercise a certain amount of discretion as to which organizations they choose to support. Obviously if the charities with which they are associated reflect their own interests then the work involved will be much more congenial. For example the lifting and preservation of the sixteenth-century warship *The Mary Rose* is a project which appeals very much to many sides of the Prince's nature – his love of history, of archaeology, of preserving our heritage and, because of the difficulties encountered in the practical side of the operation, his love of adventure and challenge.

When the Princess married she was besieged by organizations desperate for her patronage, for these days no member of the Royal Family is so guaranteed to attract a crowd and therefore raise money as the Princess of Wales. Naturally, since the couple take their connection with Wales very seriously, several of those which she finally accepted have a direct Welsh connection: she is President of the Welsh Crafts Council (rural crafts is a cause dear to the Prince's heart as well), Patron of the Welsh National Opera and Patron of the Swansea Festival of Music and the Arts. Organizations run for the benefit of children, her own major interest, account for most of her other commitments. Among other appointments she is President of the Albany Community Centre in Deptford, which is concerned with children at risk, Patron of the Malcolm Sargent Cancer Fund for Children, Patron of the Pre-School Playgroups Association (particularly appropriate for a former nursery school teacher) and Patron of the National Children's Orchestra. Most recently she has associated herself with the campaign to ensure that all potential mothers in the country are aware of the dangers of contracting German Measles in pregnancy, and are vaccinated against the disease. The influence of the Princess in areas like this is incalculable. Who knows how many people will take precautions against German Measles because the Princess of Wales advocates it? If one thing is certain, it is the press coverage that the Princess's involvement guarantees, and that will be an invaluable boost to this worthwhile campaign. To know that she may well have saved future children from being born handicapped must be a great source of satisfaction to Diana.

It is perhaps the supreme irony that Prince Charles, who has known from childhood the job he is to undertake, and has been trained to the finest detail on how to do it, still has no idea when he is to start in earnest. Most indications at the moment suggest he could be near normal retiring age before he is called on to put all the years of training to their intended use. The Queen has always been careful to avoid what she herself refers to as 'An Edward VII situation'. By that she means the predicament of Queen Victoria's eldest son who was made to wait in the wings until he was sixty years old while his mother acted out the 'dumb-show' of her public life.

OPPOSITE *Children's outfitters were taken by surprise by William's all-in-one snow suit, which ousted the traditional royal coat and bonnet. Stocks of a similar snow suit sold out in 24 hours.*

Edward's life was made virtually meaningless to him because in spite of his many talents he had no sense of purpose. To fill in his time he spent long periods holidaying and gambling and was a notorious womanizer. Edward VIII while Prince of Wales also lead a fairly feckless life. Prince Charles has a very different personality but even he, with his ability to become passionately involved in what he is doing and to construct a purpose for his life, may eventually feel that being the Queen's closest representative is not a real life for a grown man.

So the Queen's twin loyalties as mother and Sovereign are brought into conflict with each other. Remembering the shattering effect which her own father's accession had on her childhood and family life (to this day the Queen Mother feels it shortened her husband's life) she will want to allow Charles and Diana as long as possible to live a (relatively) normal family life. This is particularly important during their children's youngest, formative years. At the same time the Queen must be well aware of the dangers inherent in keeping Charles waiting another twenty or so years to be King. The spark of youth will have long since disappeared and so might the drive and enthusiasm which characterize his work at present.

With these points of view in mind many people have suggested that the Queen might abdicate in favour of her eldest son at some suitable time in the future; it has even been suggested that the Queen might follow more humble examples and retire at sixty-five. The fact that Charles now has a wife and a stable family life make him a more attractive future King than ever.

As for the Princess of Wales, it seems that in some senses she is already more popular than the Queen, not in the deep-rooted affection of the people but as a potent press image. Despite her name, which has no royal precedents, people are already finding that Queen Diana does not sound as strange as it did at first.

However, the advocates of abdication overlook the Queen's over-riding devotion to duty. She witnessed a similar life-long commitment in her father and she has seen the effect of abdication on other monarchies. When Queen Wilhelmina of the Netherlands abdicated at the age of sixty-eight in favour of her daughter Juliana, Queen Mary expressed the general contempt of the British royal ladies in declaring that sixty-eight was no age to give up one's job. Since then Juliana herself has abdicated in favour of Queen Beatrix, her own daughter, and it is a sad fact that Prince Claus, Beatrix's husband, has suffered a nervous breakdown as a result of the strains imposed on him by the premature change in his way of life. Once one partner becomes monarch the other becomes less important in what was previously an almost equal working partnership. The job of consort is a hard one, and the Queen will want to spare Diana additional burdens while her children are still young.

The Queen also realizes the value of an experienced monarch to the government of the country. Prime Ministers and governments may come and go but a long-serving sovereign can provide continuity and expertise which make the running of the country just that bit easier. She is fortunate that her eldest son agrees with her wholeheartedly in this and would certainly not want her to vacate the throne simply

In February 1984 the Princess of Wales undertook her first solo overnight engagement abroad when she visited Oslo. On her return home the news of her second pregnancy was made public.

to provide him with stable employment. He has made this abundantly clear in his own pronouncements on the subject:

I don't think monarchs should retire and be pensioned off, say, at sixty, as some professions and businesses stipulate. The nature of being a monarch is different. Take Queen Victoria. In her eighties she was more loved, more known, more revered in her country than she had ever been before. In other walks of life too age may bring accumulations of respect – and possibly wisdom – which are valuable to society.

During the course of her Jubilee year the Queen seemed to become strengthened in her resolve to continue the work in which she has been so successful. Her esteem among the Third World members of her Commonwealth is frequently greater than that of her government and her Christmas broadcast in 1983, which was devoted entirely to the problems and development of India, reflected her very personal sense of involvement. Because of this she is able to transcend the divisions within the Commonwealth, reminding all members of the common bond which unifies them.

Until now Charles has been the only one of the Queen's sons to help her with her work. In future Prince Andrew and Prince Edward will be able to relieve him and his parents of some of their royal duties, leaving Charles a little more free to pursue some of his own interests. Yet the joint appeal of the Prince and Princess of Wales is so great it is unlikely they will ever be allowed to scale down their public duties. The question is how the next twenty years will be filled, a question that perhaps applies particularly to Prince Charles, for whom the practical side of child rearing will be less of a preoccupation.

He will certainly remain firm in his commitment to projects involving young people, not only through his own Trust but as President of the United World Colleges' International Council, an educational organization of private schools from all over the world which brings together young people from many different countries. As its President Charles comes into contact with young people of different cultures on a basis which cuts through the officialdom and formalities associated with his foreign tours.

There are many people who wish that he would establish a similar position for himself as a trade ambassador for British exports abroad. Charles feels that he already makes a great effort to promote British industry wherever he goes in the world but his critics argue that his efforts would be better rewarded if he were officially engaged in some form of royal export commission. It is, however, unlikely that this will be realized.

Another project which never got off the ground was the possibility of Charles and his wife going to Australia so that Charles could spend some time as Governor-General. Although the idea may have appealed to them both personally it was not practical in political terms and was soon dropped.

When he does eventually become King he may find himself forced to make and accept changes as his mother has already done. Charles himself recognizes the need for flexibility, but in keeping with his character admits that 'rapid change is something I find difficult to keep up with.' Yet the Monarchy will have to keep pace with modern society if it is to remain secure in a world governed by mass communications, the silicon chip and the computer. The Princess of Wales who is virtually a generation younger than her husband will be able to make sure he is not left behind. Whatever *does* happen in the future Prince Charles now has the inestimable good fortune to have a wife by his side who gives him personal contentment and wonderful support in his public life.

Although in some ways his staunchly conservative ideals and behaviour seem out of keeping with the end of the twentieth century, it may well be those very characteristics which are most needed by a monarch during rapidly changing times. For the Prince and Princess of Wales – the future King and Queen – the greatest challenges lie in the future. Their first years together have given every indication that between them they have all the qualities needed to take the Monarchy into the twenty-first century. As the Prince himself says, 'It's a fascinating job, and I'm looking forward to the future.'

Diana noticeably blossomed during her tour of Australia, New Zealand and Canada. She was fortunate to be able to call on the seasoned advice and helping hand of her husband.

Acknowledgments

Photographs and illustrations are supplied or are reproduced by kind permission of the following:

The photograph on page *19* is reproduced by gracious permission of HM the Queen (Weidenfeld and Nicolson Archives)

BBC Hulton Picture Library: 24, 25, 26 (below), *36*, 42 (right)

Camera Press: half-title page (both), (left Peter Grugeon, right Snowdon), title page, centre (Snowdon), 6 (Cecil Beaton), *11*, *20* left (John Scott), 22 (Snowdon), *35* (John Scott), *40* (Snowdon), *52* (Cecil Beaton), 57, 171 (Snowdon), 185 below (Jim Bennett), 191

Central Office of Information: *122* (above right)

John Frost Historical Newspaper Service: 8 (left), *17*, *140* (right)

Tim Graham: front and back jacket, title page, facing contents page (right), 104, 112, 143 (left), 144, 148 (above left), 149 (above), 153, 154, 157, 163, 165 (right), 175 (left and right), *177*, *178*, *180*, *181*, 183, 185 above, 187 below, 189, *193*, 195

Anwar Hussein: 99 (top), *107*, *113*, *115*, *117*, *118*, 119, 121, 122 (bottom), 126, 129, 130, 131, 132, 135, *136* (left and right), 137, 139 (above and below), 141, 143, 146, 147, 148 (above right, below left and right), 149 (below), 151, 158 (below), *161* (above and below), *165* (left)

The Photo Source – Fox Photos: 32 (right), 37, 49, *55*; Keystone: 84 (right), *122* (above left); Colour Library International: 51, 62, 66, 70, 74, 76, 80–1, 82, 83, 84 (left), 87, 94, 95, 97, 98 (above and below), 102, *109*, 168, *172*, 174, 187 (above)

Photographers International: *124* (Terry Fincher)

Popperfoto: 8 (right), *14*, *15*, *18*, *20* (left), 26 (above), 28, *30–1*, 31, 32 (left), 42 (left), 44, 59, 60, 69, 72, 78 (left and right), 85 (left and right), 86, 89, 90, 92, 99 (below), *101*, *111* (left and right)

Press Association: title page (left and right), *12*, 39 (right), 47, 64, *133*, *140* (left), *158* (above)

Rex Features: contents page (far right) 166, 167

Syndication International: 39 (left)

Designed by Allison Waterhouse
Picture research by Lucy Shankleman
Numbers in italic indicate black and white illustrations.

Index